LAW AND
LIBERTY

The Alan Redpath Library

ALAN REDPATH

LAW AND LIBERTY

THE TEN COMMANDMENTS FOR TODAY

Fleming H. Revell
A Division of Baker Book House Co
Grand Rapids, Michigan 49516

Library of Congress Cataloging-in-Publication Data
Redpath, Alan.
    Law and liberty.

    1.   Commandments, Ten.   2.   Christian life—
1960-   I.   Bible.   O. T.   Exodus xx, 1-17.   English.
1978.   II.   Title.
BV4655.R4   241.5'2   77-14980
ISBN 0-8007-5515-4

TO *the student body of Capernwray Bible School,*
England, who have been at the receiving end of
much of the contents of this volume, with deep
gratitude to the Lord for the privilege of ministry to
them . . .

Contents

Preface

In my younger life I benefited greatly from the teaching of Dr. G. Campbell Morgan, whose ministry, among others, was used of God to cause me to leave business and enter the Lord's service. Not surprisingly, therefore, much of what he said and taught has found its way into my own preaching and writing, and in fact spurred me on in the first place to declare the relevance of the Ten Commandments for today in pastoral ministry, and latterly in teaching at the Capernwray Bible School, of which I am now pastoral dean.

The students there have often requested the lectures I gave them to be put into print. This I have now done—not by any means word for word, but revised and edited so that this book expresses, as best I know how, some of the major things that have burdened my heart as a preacher of the gospel throughout my life.

The whole world is desperately searching for freedom, and the Christian alone has the answer, namely submission to Jesus as Lord, that through His life the righteousness of the Law might be expressed in him by the Spirit. This is the thrust of this little volume. My earnest prayer is that it may become the inspiration of many a reader, who will make the great discovery that liberty and license are poles apart, and true liberty is only through obedience to the Lord's commands in the power of His Spirit.

I am deeply indebted to my beloved wife for the many hours of help in typing and checking the proofs and also to Mr. and Mrs. Gordon Randall of Florida, who were instrumental in arranging the preparation of the manuscript from tapes.

ALAN REDPATH

Willow Beck Cottage,
Capernwray Hall,
Carnforth, Lancashire

1

The First Commandment:

WHO IS YOUR GOD?

I am the Lord your God, who brought you out of the land of Egypt, out of the house of slavery. You shall have no other gods before Me. (Exodus 20:2, 3)

Probably it is necessary at the outset of a series of studies of this character to clear an acre of ground, if you know what I mean. First of all, I would dispose of one line of thought concerning the teaching of the Ten Commandments. In the thinking of some people they have no significance today whatsoever. They were given to the Jews, and their impact is therefore purely national and dispensational. With the close of the Old Testament dispensation and the introduction of this age of grace, when God deals with men in grace and not in judgment, they have no place whatever. Now I believe that such teaching is not only highly dangerous but totally unbiblical.

Let me remind you that spiritual principles are abiding. An overemphasis on dispensationalism can overlook that fact. You cut some slices from a cake, but they are still part of the whole cake; and in the same way history is an organic whole which cannot be neatly dissected.

Let me put three passages from the Word of God together so that they can be seen side by side:

> And you shall remember all the way which the Lord your God has led you in the wilderness these forty years, that He might humble you, testing you, to know what was in your heart, whether you would keep His commandments or not. And He humbled you and let you be hungry, and fed you with manna which you did not

know, nor did your fathers know, that He might make
you understand that man does not live by bread alone,
but man lives by everything that proceeds out of the
mouth of the Lord.

Deuteronomy 8:2, 3

Then in Matthew 4:4 is the tremendous account of the attack
in the wilderness upon our Lord by the devil, when He coun-
terattacked with the words, "It is written, 'MAN SHALL NOT LIVE
ON BREAD ALONE, BUT ON EVERY WORD THAT PROCEEDS OUT OF
THE MOUTH OF GOD.' "

Do not think that I came to abolish the Law or the
Prophets; I did not come to abolish, but to fulfill. For
truly I say to you, until heaven and earth pass away, not
the smallest letter or stroke shall pass away from the Law,
until all is accomplished. Whosoever then annuls one of
the least of these commandments, and so teaches others,
shall be called least in the kingdom of heaven; but whoever keeps and teaches them, he shall be called great in
the kingdom of heaven. For I say to you, that unless your
righteousness surpasses that of the scribes and
Pharisees, you shall not enter the kingdom of heaven.

Matthew 5:17–20

Now what to your mind do those passages in God's Word
teach? Surely this, that your life and mine are perfectly con-
ditioned only when they are governed by the words that pro-
ceed from the mouth of God. The creation and preservation and
ritual of the Hebrew people—and in particular the Law given to
them—were directed to the end of expressing God's intention
for their happiness in receiving His law from His mouth, and
giving unquestioned obedience to it. Today, in a world that has
lost its bearings tragically, the Ten Commandments are an
orientation course which speaks with final authority. God Himself is the supreme orientation point, and therefore the first four
Commandments have to do with our relationship to Him. All
other relationships in life depend upon these.

God's first order for all time is the family, therefore that is the
subject of the Fifth Commandment. In society one has to show
love to other people, and respect the rights of individuals, so

there are Commandments Six, Seven, Eight, Nine. In the case of each person, all unsatisfied longings poison every relationship of life, therefore the Tenth Commandment is given.

Thus this important section of the Word of God is what I would call "an orientation course," with the Lord the supreme center, followed by relationship to the family, society, and finally oneself.

The Lord Jesus lived His life constantly, without exception, by the words which proceeded from the mouth of His Father. When He died on Calvary He bore the penalty of man's disobedience to God's law. He rose from the dead, and took up His life again because of His obedience: "For this reason the Father loves Me, because I lay down My life that I may take it again. No one has taken it away from Me, but I lay it down on My own initiative. I have authority to lay it down, and I have authority to take it up again. This commandment I received from My Father" (John 10:17, 18).

Jesus Christ took up His life again that He might communicate that life to us, in order that by His energy and power we might fulfill the law of God. Romans 8, of course, is the prime classic on that, and I quote the first four verses:

> There is therefore now no condemnation for those who are in Christ Jesus. For the law of the Spirit of life in Christ Jesus has set you free from the law of sin and of death. For what the Law could not do, weak as it was through the flesh, God did: sending His own Son in the likeness of sinful flesh and as an offering for sin, He condemned sin in the flesh, in order that the requirement of the Law might be fulfilled in us, who do not walk according to the flesh, but according to the Spirit.

The whole genius of Calvary is to end rebellion and put submission back where it belongs. I hope we recognize that and understand it.

When we pray: "Our Father, who art in heaven, hallowed be Thy Name. Thy kingdom come . . ." *hold it right there.* You cannot pray "Thy kingdom come" until you have prayed "my kingdom go." To be a Christian is the end of the rule of one kingdom and the beginning of a new regime. The kingdom of darkness becomes the kingdom of light. The kingdom of Satan in my heart becomes the Kingdom of God. Calvary, in its genius and purpose, is to end rebellion and begin submission. The new life of the Holy Spirit, which we receive at our new birth, must be regulated by a holiness expressed in the Ten Commandments. An outward profession of faith must be backed by an inward practice of a holy life.

Now I hope I will not be misunderstood when I say with all my heart that I believe it is not more truth we need to know primarily, but 100 percent obedience to what we already know. The gospel is not an easy way of escape from God's law. It is His plan whereby His law can be fulfilled in the life of every believer. Therefore, these ten words are the words of God uttered for the government of a people (first of all the Jewish nation and then ourselves) whose glory would lie in their absolute obedience to Him and to His Word, and whose constant shame would lie in their revolt against His authority.

These Ten Commandments, of course, presuppose sin. They will have no place in heaven, for the nature that we will have there will put disobedience beyond any possibility at all. But as long as you live here, whether you are a Christian or not, you are living in constant touch with a nature that is sinful, and it is never God's plan to improve that nature, or to make you better. It is His purpose to condemn that nature at the cross and replace it with Jesus. God is not in the self-improvement plan: He is in the "Christ-replacement" plan. That thrills my heart! And it is of tremendous importance, for we need to be reminded that though the law of the Spirit of life in Christ sets us free from the law of sin and death, it does not set us free from the law of God. Liberty is not being away on our own somewhere marked "independent." That is not liberty but lawlessness that can lead to license. Liberty is fulfilling our destiny to do the will of God. Liberty, therefore, leads to law. Indeed, you will remember that James in his letter speaks about the law of liberty in 1:25.

> But one who looks intently at the perfect law, the law of liberty, and abides by it, not having become a forgetful hearer but an effectual doer, this man shall be blessed in what he does.

Perhaps I can define law this way, that it is a rule laid down by one intelligent being to another, the one having a right to exercise his authority over the other. Now if anyone tells me that savors of legalism, I say, "Blessed legalism!" It is the kind of authority I need in my life twenty-four hours a day, the absolute sovereignty of Jesus as Lord.

Augustine said, "Love God and do as you like." Yes, because love transforms His law into liberty: a law of liberty. "Take My yoke upon you, and learn from Me . . . . For My yoke is easy [My yoke fits], and My load is light" (Matthew 11:29, 30). It is wonderfully true that the gospel does not demand that we, by our own effort, keep the law of God. The Law fills us with helplessness, because by the Law is the knowledge of sin "that every mouth may be closed" (Romans 3:19). The Law opens our eyes and shuts our mouth. It leaves us without excuse. It drives us to Jesus. It is our schoolmaster to lead us to Christ, and when we come to Him in absolute helplessness and hopelessness in ourselves, we find that every word of the Law is repeated and emphasized in the Christian economy.

The Ten Commandments are all interpreted in the Sermon on the Mount and amplified in the Lord's teaching there, when He preached not to unconverted people but to His disciples (*see* Matthew 5:1, 2). It is the kind of life God expects people born of His Spirit, indwelt by His life, to live in the world today so that men, in a society that has lost its bearings, may see the sheer thrill of a life lived under the dominion of the Lord Jesus Christ.

"Why should that be?" you ask. Because the severity of the law of God is the most wonderful expression of His love. You see, our God is set upon our perfection. We are saved that we might be conformed to the image of Christ. He wants to make us like Him, and if He excused sin or condoned it, it would be absolutely impossible to fulfill that objective. The cross frees us from the Law's condemnation, but it does not free us from obligation. Jesus alive today is the One who has the right to rule my life, and the Holy Spirit in my heart comes to apply that rule every day. Every demand that God makes upon me is met by the Spirit in me in answer to my faith, submission, yieldedness. He it is who gives me the power to obey, "for it is God who is at work in you, both to will and to work for His good pleasure" (Philippians 2:13).

So having cleared some ground, we turn to this First Commandment, the first of four which have to do with our relationship with God. This Commandment brings us face to face with the object of our worship: "I am the Lord your God, who brought you out of the land of Egypt, out of the house of slavery. You shall have no other gods before Me."

Do you notice that the strongest argument for obedience is the experience of our past deliverance? How that should ring a bell in your heart when you think of your past deliverance at Calvary, where His blood was shed!

Right away, here at the beginning, God confronts us with Himself by the name *Jehovah*. This is a combination of three words meaning "He that is, He that will be, and He that was." At once we are brought into the presence of the supreme, eternal God. If I reach out into the unknown future that has no ending, "I am He that will be." If I think of the present moment of life, with all its problems, its mystery, and all the things I don't understand and find hard to cope with, "I am He that is." If I think back into the infinite past, God says, "I am He that was." Whether we think of our origin, our present condition today, or our future, He says, "I AM." I don't think any of us can escape that immense revelation of a covenant-keeping God, Jehovah, who never breaks His word.

He says, "I am Jehovah, thy God." The second word is *Elohim,* meaning "the supreme object of worship, the absolutely omnipotent God." "I am Jehovah, thy God"—and upon that fact rests this First Commandment: "You shall have no other gods before Me." Of course, if He is what He claims to be, what a very unreasonable thing it would be to have any other god in my life before Him. There cannot be two people who fulfill that description of omnipotence. Any other god must be limited.

There is something here, too, about the necessity of worship. Every man must have a god. There is really no such person as an atheist, for such a man worships himself and the material world. There is no human being without a shrine in his heart where there is a god whom he worships. The very composition of human life demands a center of worship as a necessity of existence. The question is, Who is *your* god? I wonder if in the presence of the living Lord Jesus you can answer that question to Him personally.

I would not know who your God is, but I could tell you who mine is, and I think you could go with me along this line, because our God is the person we think most precious, for whom we would make the greatest sacrifice, and who moves our hearts with the warmest love. He is the person who, if we lost Him, would leave us desolate. If we possess Him, then we are blessed indeed. I repeat, who is *your* God?

Now here in this First Commandment is a declaration that at the very center of our lives there has to be enthroned not a rabble of little gods, not a hypothetical, unknowable being, but a living person who can arrange our program, utter His command, and expect obedience: the living God. At the very center of life there must be one Lord, Jesus Christ. If a person is governed by many lords then he is in bondage to them all, and desolated and confused by their conflicting claims. If a multitude of things are making a claim upon his life for preeminence, he is in a state of jitters all the time, wondering to which one he should yield. But when that man yields to Jesus as Lord, he is released from every other kind of captivity. You see, you and I are free only when we are not free to be free of God. Let that sink in until you can really say in all truth, "Amen!"

Like many people today I have to do a lot of plane travel, and while I am not exactly fearful I am always very prayerful! It never ceases to amaze me that a Jumbo Jet weighing half a million pounds can ever get off the ground. Loaded with some 380 passengers, baggage, and fuel, it sits on the runway like an immense static object, and it passes the knowledge of the average person how such a weight can ever be raised in the air. There it sits, held close to the ground by the irrevocable law of gravity. But once the captain starts the engines and the giant plane trundles along the runway, something begins to happen. He revs the engines until the roar is deafening, and the plane moves faster and faster until it reaches a certain speed; then he points the nose of the plane up into the air, and it begins to rise, up and up, until it reaches its estimated height, and it is on its way. What now has happened to the law of gravity? Does it cease to work? No, but a new law has taken over, the law of aerodynamics, which now has power over the law of gravity and enables that plane to remain airborne. Of course, at any moment the laws could be reversed—if the engines failed, for example—when at once the law of gravity would come into operation again, and the plane would plummet to the ground.

But mercifully that happens very rarely, and the mighty power of aerodynamics sets the plane free from the equally mighty power of gravity.

Now I tell you all this to remind you of a tremendous principle which is the genius of the gospel. Paul outlines it in Romans 8:2: "For the law of the Spirit of life in Christ Jesus has set you free from the law of sin and of death." Yes, the law of the Spirit of life in Christ Jesus holds me like a vise and lifts me up above the downward pull of degeneration, placing me under the law of the upward pull of regeneration, for Jesus Christ sets me free. What a glorious truth, and what a precious experience! For we are free only when we are not free to be free of God, for He must govern every aspect of our lives.

If that is the secret of living, it is also the genesis of idolatry; that is what makes idolatry possible. From the moment a man loses the vision of the One who says "I am Jehovah, the Lord, your God," at that moment he puts something else in His place.

The gods of the heathen, both in Bible times and today, are many. In Old Testament times there were those with whose names you will be familiar—Moloch, Baal, Mammon. To worship Moloch was to descend to cruelty. He was the god of the Ammonites (*see* Leviticus 20). To worship Baal, which means "possessor," was to descend to being an animal or a beast. Second Kings 10 gives an example of that. To worship Mammon was to worship carnality.

Now these gods go by other names, of course, but do I need to tell you that they are with us yet? How many people in the world today just don't care two cents how other people live or die, as long as they get their own end? That is the ruthless method of the communists, where everything is sacrificed for the state, and they are willing to sacrifice millions of lives to establish their goals, for in their eyes the end justifies the means. That is why in industry there are strikes, lockouts, hospitals cut down, medical service refused, even in emergency cases. Yes, in our country even doctors and nurses have been on strike. That is why it is never known whether a train will run on time, or if it will run at all! That is why the auto industry is in the mess it is, caused by a few men who go straight for their own goal at any price. This is the worship of the god Moloch modern style.

Then again, how many women are there on the streets of

every city in the world today because of the god Baal? While most people have to go through the doctor's office and then the drugstore to get a prescription, any teenage girl can go straight into a drugstore and get contraceptives on demand. This is sex on the state, the worship of the god Baal. Of course this evil promiscuity is seen in other areas of life, and is now penetrating our homes through the TV set. There is a fight on the hands of every Christian to attempt to thwart this, because it all points to the fact that when man has lost his vision of a holy God, he worships impurity. Alas that his zeal in perpetrating this evil is at times more vigorous than the passion of the believer for those who are lost and therefore sucked down by the evil around them.

How many people imagine that life consists of the abundance of things they possess, though they are getting a bit of a shock these days! This is the worship of Mammon, and the First Commandment needs to be preached with new force to every worshiper at his shrine. The Lord Jesus said, "No one can serve two masters; for either he will hate the one and love the other, or he will hold to one and despise the other. You cannot serve God and Mammon" (Matthew 6:24).

In the New Testament we have a picture of the end product: "For many walk, of whom I often told you, and now tell you even weeping, that they are enemies of the cross of Christ, whose end is destruction, whose god is their appetite, and whose glory is in their shame, who set their minds on earthly things" (Philippians 3:18, 19).

Here is the god of animal appetite: what we shall eat, what we shall wear, how we will satisfy the cravings of our carnal mind. Indeed, we are compelled to realize that this is the god of *myself*. You probably have different problems, but my main problem is with myself, because while the Lord Jesus has taken all of myself to the cross, I still have to live with myself every day, and so does my wife. There is the god of "me, my, mine, I" that hates being criticized, which likes to be thought well of by other people, which can be very resentful. The only reason why so many Christians never become involved in "full-time" service (or even offer for work in their local church) is that they worship the god of self—self-preservation. They are touchy, resentful, easily hurt, and have no wish to take the rap for their behavior from fellow believers, so often you find them on the

sidelines criticizing what their colleagues are doing for the
Lord. It is a true but terrifying thought that a person can attend
church and worship every Sunday, but in fact be an idolator.

Let us consider finally the cost of worship. We have thought
about the necessity of worship, and the object of worship, but
we find that God has not set aside the Law, as I have said, but
has found a way by which His people can fulfill it; therefore
there is a cost to our worship. He has not given up the claim to
worship and said that His people can have other gods. No, for
the Lord Jesus said in Matthew 22:37, "YOU SHALL LOVE THE
LORD YOUR GOD WITH ALL YOUR HEART, AND WITH ALL YOUR
SOUL, AND WITH ALL YOUR MIND." Furthermore we read, "Then
Jesus said to His disciples, 'If any one wishes to come after Me,
let him deny himself, and take up his cross, and follow Me' "
(Matthew 16:24).

What a tragic divorce it is in the character of God to suggest
that one can have Jesus as Saviour and not as Lord. You cannot.
He is Lord and then He is Saviour. There must be a moment in
the life of a child of God when he gets off the throne and kneels
there in order to enthrone the Lord Jesus.

But worship costs everything. Worship permits of no substitute. The Lord pointed this out to the woman of Samaria when
He said to her, "An hour is coming, and now is, when the true
worshipers shall worship the Father in spirit and truth; for such
people the Father seeks to be His worshipers" (John 4:23). In
effect He was saying to the woman, "My dear woman, it is not a
question of location, of place, or denomination; it is a question
of your heart being open to reality."

The risen Lord said the same thing to the church at Ephesus,
which thought it was so sound, so orthodox and correct, so
separatist, who would not allow anything in that was the least
bit suspicious, and yet His verdict was, "But I have this against
you, that you have left your first love" (Revelation 2:4).

A man once came to me and told me he had just celebrated
his silver wedding. He said he had been worried about his wife
for the past ten years, for although he had given her so much—a
new car every other year, all the clothes she needed, refur-
nished the house whenever she suggested it—yet she was cold
and unresponsive, and the poor man was painfully puzzled. So
on their anniversary he took her out to a lovely dinner, and
when she was thoroughly relaxed he plucked up courage to say

to her, "Honey, we have been married twenty-five years today, and you have been a wonderful person. I want to thank you for being my wife, but for the last ten years I have been so concerned, for in spite of all the things I have given you—cars, clothes, new homes, and so on—you have been so distant and unresponsive. Please tell me why this is."

Her reply was, "I am so glad you have asked me that, because I have been wanting to tell you but have not dared. I am so grateful for all you have given me through the years, and I have loved everything. But, you know, for so many years you have never given me the love of your heart."

The man told me just how he felt, and you can imagine it too.

"I have somewhat against you, you have abandoned the love you had at the first."

It is so easy to give the Lord work, time, money, things—but how long is it since you told Jesus you love Him? Where does He come in your love life: first, second, third, or one of the also-rans?

Worship permits no substitute and demands all that a person has. For the woman of Samaria as well as the church in Ephesus it was "repent, change your direction . . . or else." To the woman the Lord said, "Go, call your husband, then come." To the church of Ephesus He said, "Remember . . . repent . . . or else I am coming to you . . . ."

Let us hear what the Spirit says to the churches, and if He has one thing to say to the Church today it is "change"—repent and make room for the love of God; and this demands everything that every believer in every church has got, in presenting himself, his time, his intensity, his possessions—all and everything. For true worship is manifested through all one's heart, all one's soul, and all one's mind: there is no shortcut, and there is no substitute.

2

The Second Commandment:
GODLY JEALOUSY

I am the Lord your God, who brought you out of the land of Egypt, out of the house of slavery. You shall have no other gods before Me. You shall not make for yourself an idol, or any likeness of what is in heaven above or on the earth beneath or in the water under the earth. You shall not worship them or serve them; for I, the Lord your God, am a jealous God, visiting the iniquity of the fathers on the children, on the third and the fourth generations of those who hate Me, but showing lovingkindness to thousands, to those who love Me and keep My commandments. (Exodus 20:2–6)

You and I live in a world in revolt. Until a year or two ago, never had a generation ever had so much, grumbled so continually, and sought so constantly for more. But those days are over. No longer is it the affluent society. Now the problem is that of survival. A society which is brilliant enough to put men on the moon, to relay by satellite all round the world events live on television, yet in trying to settle its racial, industrial, and economic problems by riots, strikes, assassinations, has gone stark, staring mad.

Once upon a time, not so long ago, the United Nations was a hope for peace. But that has been reduced to sheer impotence through Vietnam and events in the Middle East. Universities today seek to assert a role, to be in a critical position in the center of our society, but the moral vacuum that exists right there erases the Ten Commandments altogether.

Now, of course, we Christians love to get together and lament all that, and almost enjoy speaking about it as we link it with the Lord's return. But shame on us—we don't do a thing about it, perhaps because we just don't know what to do. We like living in our cozy little circles, and it may well be that the sin of this age will be the blindness and heartlessness of Christian people who leave others out there somewhere because they just do not know how to cope with them. Let's face it: so many Christians don't want to get involved with people. They are prepared to do a bit of evangelism and hand out literature and so on, but they don't want really to become involved where people are.

I believe we are finished, absolutely finished, if this generation does not seek the will of God afresh in society, and realize His purpose in sending Jesus is expressed in these Commandments. There is a madness in our world which God wants to deal with, and because we are in the world He wants to begin with us. So I believe the time has come for Christian revolution. It is the only revolution that has a chance. Every human revolt begins from the outside and never touches the center. It can achieve a great deal, but it cannot change the human heart. Christian revolt starts from the center and ought to work right out to the circumference. A Christian is one who has revolted against himself by dethroning himself and enthroning Jesus to set up the Kingdom of God in his life.

In the Ten Commandments and the Sermon on the Mount we find the terms for citizens of God's kingdom. When a Christian discovers that, he is meant to be a part of a redeemed humanity which owns Jesus Christ as Lord to demonstrate to this crazy world that the freedom and joy and liberty of life are found in total submission to Jesus Christ as Lord. That is why I find these days so exciting to live in.

So, with that introduction, we are going to consider this very interesting and challenging Second Commandment. Now the First Commandment forbids us to have any other gods beside the One who has made Himself known by the name Jehovah. This second one assumes the existence of God, but forbids the creation of any material thing supposed to represent Him in order to assist us to worship. Now at first sight you might feel that there is not much danger of any of us getting into trouble with this one, and perhaps the preacher should go to some ritualistic church in order that he might preach it there. Not a bit of it! I think that by the time we are through, you will feel that we are in grave danger in our own lives in unexpected areas of breaking this law.

First of all, let us be quite sure that we understand this command and the necessity for it. The force of it lies in the closing words: "You shall not make for yourself an idol, or any likeness of what is in heaven above or on the earth beneath or in the water under the earth. You shall not worship them or serve them."

You see, a man declares that he must have something to help him in the worship of God. A devout Roman Catholic says he does not worship the image but the God behind it. He doesn't worship the crucifix, but it helps him to think about Jesus. Now that is exactly what God forbids. Not that a man should not actually worship a crucifix, but that he should not use a crucifix to help him to worship the Lord.

Now why should that be? You may think it is very unreasonable of the Lord, but it is not: "God is spirit; and those who worship Him must worship in spirit and truth" (John 4:24). The material cannot possibly help the spiritual. Something which a fallen man creates cannot help him in the worship of the God who created it. The spiritual sense in man is dead because of sin.

When we arrived in this world as little babies we were only two-thirds alive. We had physical life and mental life, but we had no spiritual life. It is a strange thing that unconverted people often say the Christian "isn't all there." Bless their hearts, it is they who are not all there—they are only two-thirds alive! The Christian has come alive. He is altogether alive because he possesses life on a new dimension—spiritual life. A man who knows God, who has experienced the new birth, and who is living in fellowship with Him, does not need any image to help him to pray. By the new birth our spiritual consciousness is restored, and we each of us have direct access to God through Jesus. Now if a man seeks the help of an image, it proves that he has no inner spiritual life. Therefore he cannot possibly create anything which can give a true representation of God. When God gave this command it was because He knew that if a man sets up an image when he has no sense of His presence, no communion with Him, that will lead that man to have a false conception of what God is really like. If the image is false, the thought of God is false, and that produces character which is also false.

You recall the language of Psalms 115:6, 8, where it says, speaking of idols, "They have ears, but they cannot hear; they have noses, but they cannot smell . . . . Those who make them will become like them . . . ."

A man becomes like the thing he worships. If he puts anything in the place of God, he ultimately becomes like it. Isn't that what Christianity is all about, that daily I might be less like myself and more like Jesus? That is the goal of Christian living. Therefore this command is not to restrict but to save us from eternal harm and loss, from having a false conception of what God is like, and becoming like that which is false.

Now how do you think we are in danger of breaking this law today? I will mention some different ways. First (and very unlikely, perhaps, in your context), by the use of the priesthood. Wherever someone bares his soul to a priest because he imagines he is getting to know God through him, he is in danger of making that priest an idol, and the result is degradation of worship.

Dr. Donald Barnhouse, formerly minister of the Tenth Presbyterian Church in Philadelphia, used to be a favorite speaker at the English Keswick Convention. Each day he would walk to the tent where the meetings were held, from his hotel, along a footpath through a field, and he would pass a Roman Catholic priest, and they said good morning to each other. One day they stopped and had a chat, and Dr. Barnhouse said to the priest, "Tell me, why do you worship the Virgin Mary? What is the idea? Why do you seek to approach God through her?"

"It is like this," said the priest. "Suppose I want to get an interview with the king. Of course, that would be very bold, as I don't know him, so I think I would go to the prime minister first and ask him if he could get me an introduction. You see, that is the idea."

"All right, that is very nice," Dr. Barnhouse replied, "but suppose the king is my father. I am not going to waste time seeing the prime minister and asking him if I can have a chat with my father!"

Yes, every one of us as Christians has a direct right of access to God through the blood of Jesus.

Another way in which this command is broken is through a

very ritualistic form of service which is supposed to create conditions conducive to worship. What is the result? Do people who worship that way become more spiritual? Do they reveal more of Jesus, more of the fruit of the Spirit? I respectfully question it. Ritualism is very refined, but it begins and ends with the senses, and it cannot possibly save.

Another way in which we are in danger of breaking this command is not by the crucifix, or an image, or the priesthood, but in our own mind. The images a man makes are not always on the walls of a temple or a house, but on the walls of the mind, graven there, secretly worshiped. Unholy desires, impure thoughts are often the secret idols. They are not something we create to help us to God, but something which seems to take God's place and therefore makes real worship impossible. The graven image of imagination before which we bow down and serve is a very real menace.

Satan's weapons are geared to prevent worship, and he attacks the mind to keep us away from the Lord. Sinful thoughts are not, of course, in themselves sin. It is what we do with them that matters. People say one to another, "That thought passed through my mind." Well, that is fine—just chase it through! Let it pass. But the trouble is that that is not always accomplished, and very often a sinful thought attacks through eyegate or eargate and is given houseroom. Satan is at his work every day, all the time, and a thought is cherished and indulged in until a graven image is carved upon the mind. I find that such a graven image can be carried from the secret chamber of my mind, from the privacy of my home, to the publicity of the street. It can haunt and invade imagination at every moment, and which of us does not know times when even the moments which we would keep as the holiest of all in our personal quiet time and devotion are invaded with sinful thoughts? Therefore before this law we all stand condemned.

I have briefly described what I suggest is the battle of every Christian's life, if we are honest and prepared to admit it—the moments of our quiet time, the times when we have been reading God's Word, when suddenly Satan has flooded us with all kinds of things of which we are ashamed. So often we have carried them from the secret place with God out into the public, and we find ourselves defeated and bogged down, and we loathe ourselves for it. To find the answer to all this, we need to read what follows the giving of this Commandment in Exodus 20:5: "I, the Lord your God, am a jealous God."

Can that be? Isn't jealousy about the worst thing imaginable when it gets hold of a person? It is the seed of murder. It leads to all kinds of broken relationships. What a hateful thing jealousy is! But here I read this striking phrase, "I, the Lord your God, am a jealous God." Let us therefore try to understand the meaning of the word.

I would say to you that God's jealousy is love in action. He refuses to share the human heart with any rival, not because He is selfish and wants us all for Himself, but because He knows that upon that loyalty to Him depends our very moral life. There is no happiness without holiness, and God is fearful lest His people bestow their affections somewhere else, on some other master. Our maturity, our happiness, our usefulness, are bound up all together with our faithfulness to Him. How anxiously the Lord surveys our actions, thoughts, desires—all because of His tremendous concern for our welfare. God is not jealous *of* us: He is jealous *for* us.

If you want the proof of that, think for a moment of Calvary. Instead of striking down the rebel and putting an end to humanity, who had revolted against Him, God allows Himself to be murdered by the rebel, in order to win back his love. God's jealousy is love in action. It is love's greatest flame.

What an example you have of it in the apostle Paul, who writes to the Corinthian church, "I am jealous for you with a godly jealousy . . ." (2 Corinthians 11:2). What a contrast from the day when he went down from Jerusalem to Damascus, and in the course of the journey had a confrontation with the risen Lord. He embarked on that journey because he was jealous: he was afraid of his position as a member of the Sanhedrin. He felt that these believers were taking away all his power and authority, and he had a commission from the high priest to kill as many as he could lay his hands on. Paul was eaten up with jealousy, until he met Jesus. He had been jealous of the believers, but now he writes to the church at Corinth, "I am jealous for you with a godly jealousy."

You know, it is a wonderful thing when a person is jealous, and then that jealousy is not just destroyed but transformed. Are you a jealous kind of person, jealous of other people? Well, here is the miracle that only the gospel can achieve, to take a jealous person and absolutely revolutionize him by making him jealous *for* people for their good and for their welfare. Paul said again, "My children, with whom I am again in labor until Christ is formed in you . . ." (Galatians 4:19). Paul—who was once jealous *of* people—is now jealous *for* them!

When the Lord Jesus gets hold of us like that, and His Holy Spirit really works in our hearts, we begin to care, and want to be involved and love people to Christ.

What a tremendous revelation there is in this Commandment of the character of God. He is a jealous God, but not only so: He is a just God. In Exodus 20:5, 6 it is stated that if a man puts something in the place of his Creator, that sin is visited upon his family. False worship of a false God tends to be handed down to the next generation. It is a solemn thing to pass on to our children a wrong conception of the Lord. I wonder what images we as parents have worshiped that have become the gods of our children. What thoughts and desires have we transmitted to the next generation? What father has not lived to see, to his shame, his children worshiping the false gods that he himself showed them?

A couple had a child who was terribly crippled from birth, and they were desperate. So the father took his child to every doctor imaginable, but they could do nothing for her. Eventually he heard of some specialist who was supposed to be the best in the nation for this particular trouble, and he took his daughter to see him, which involved him in a very high fee. The consultant examined her very carefully, and then said to the father, "I am sorry, but I cannot do anything for her." The man lost his temper. "What's the use of going to you specialists? Here am I paying all this money just for the pleasure of being told you can't do a thing for her! What's the use of that?" The specialist turned to him and said, "Sir, I was going to spare you, but you have been straight with me, and I must be equally frank with you. I have a feeling that the condition of your child is very probably due to the kind of life you lived before you were married."

The Lord is a just God. What a solemn thing that is, "visiting the iniquity of the fathers on the children, on the third and the fourth generation . . . ."

But see, if He is a just God, how merciful He is. What a wonderful promise there is here, "showing lovingkindness to thousands." Or, as another rendering puts it, "showing mercy unto a thousand generations of them that love me." God visits the iniquity to three or four generations, but He shows mercy to thousands.

If I am prepared to sweep away those idols and get into living touch with the Lord, my life can influence not only this generation but the next. God calls each one of us into His presence to worship Him, not to listen to sermons or music, but to get far beyond that, to come face to face with the living Lord Jesus. Whenever we stop short of that we have stopped short of worship. But we need not stop short there, for in Hebrews 10:19, 20 we read that believers can come boldly into His presence through the blood of Jesus, through the veil that has been rent in two. The priesthood has been done away, and a direct path has been made into His presence for everyone through the shed blood of the Lord Jesus Christ, without preacher or prophet or priest. Every person can go right in to worship Him.

This is the only answer to the images on the mind, to press home to the presence of God and plead with Him for deliverance. My friend, you can have as much of God as you want. In fact, you never have any more. He is never off duty. He is never unavailable. He has no consulting hours. Twenty-four hours, day or night, He is always available, and when the enemy comes into the mind like a flood, He can raise a standard against him. So often, alas, we lie down to these idols; we don't show God that we mean business in getting rid of them but often seem so content to live with them.

I read these statistics recently, which struck me very forcefully: In the average Christian life of 75 years, we spend 25 years asleep, 18 years at work, 6 years traveling, 7½ years dressing, 9 years watching TV, 6 years eating, 4 years being sick, and 6 months in devotion. Does that hit you as it hit me? If I am appalled by the graven images that come into my mind, if I am determined in the name of the Lord to get rid of them, I have to show God that I mean business with Him.

This is a very personal question, but it demands an answer: How many hours sleep do you—not want, but—*need?* Eight hours? That means if you live to be 75 you will have spent 25 years unconscious, ignorant of all that is going on! If you cut one hour of that you would have 3½ years more for prayer. I think that is worth considering seriously.

You and I are engaged in a warfare that will never end until we meet Jesus face to face—total, absolute, all-out war. We are faced with a mighty foe who is the greatest power in the universe, bar One, and that One is Jesus. If I seek Him earnestly with all my heart, I will surely find Him. But if I allow my devotional life to be purely formal, if I skimp Bible study and prayer, I will find I am living my life with a graven image on my mind, and prayer becomes impossible.

When I was younger I used to play Rugby football and was very keen and active. Because I was big and strong I got on better than some, and I played for one of our English counties. When the football season began I got up every morning about 6 A.M. and ran for about ten miles round a suburb of London before going to business. Then in the evening I went to a running track to run another ten miles. That was about twenty miles a day, five days a week! When I finished that I did a period of skipping, then I put on football gear, and back at the house where I stayed I would go to a corner of a wall and push with one shoulder hard. Then I would change to the other corner and the other shoulder, and shoved until the pain was fearful! Nobody was looking, except my landlady, who thought I was absolutely mad! But I was determined that when I turned out on a Saturday afternoon to play football, anyone hitting me would hit a lump of concrete, and he would not want to do it again! It worked pretty well too!

Now if I am prepared to do all that for football, how much more am I prepared to do for Jesus? To quote 1 Corinthians 9:26, 27 in *The Living Bible* paraphrase, "So I run straight to the goal with purpose in every step. I fight to win. I'm not just shadow-boxing or playing around. Like an athlete I punish my body, treating it roughly, training it to do what it should, not what it wants to . . . ."

What we need every day is *blanket victory*—the ability to get out of bed, into a shower, then to read the Word of God and meet Him in prayer, asking Him that for that day and every day He will give deliverance from the graven images on the mind. You see, to worship Him in spirit means to be prepared to forsake every idol in one's heart. Are you? Or do you love it more than you love Jesus? Are you really 100 percent willing to declare war on sin, or have you reservations?

I wonder what image has been erected in your mind that is

between you and the Lord now, and at what point you are breaking this command every day. Are you willing for every idol to be torn down? You see, only the Holy Spirit can do this, for His action in your heart depends upon your attitude to Jesus. If you reject Him on this issue, the Holy Spirit at once convicts you. If you yield to Him, then the Holy Spirit will fill you. If you obey Him, then the Holy Spirit will use you. How determined are you that God will give you deliverance, when for years your whole Christian testimony has been dragged down and spoiled because of a graven image in your life?

Thank God that if we confess our sin He is faithful and just to forgive us and cleanse us from all unrighteousness (*see* 1 John 1:9). Thank God that the law of the spirit of life that has been set loose in our hearts sets us free from the law of sin and death. Thank God, too, in the words of 2 Corinthians 10:4, 5, that "the weapons of our warfare are not of the flesh, but divinely powerful for the destruction of fortresses. We are destroying speculations and every lofty thing raised up against the knowledge of God, and we are taking every thought captive to the obedience of Christ."

You see, therefore, the reason for God's jealousy: worship is all or nothing. To offer less than all involves us in slavery. To give Him all means liberty.

How graphically that great Russian Christian philosopher, Alexander Solzhenitsyn, gives expression to all of this, in different words and context, of course, in an article published recently in the Paris paper *Le Point:*

> You think now only of a liberty without duties and without responsibilities which ends up as nothing more than enjoying material things. You are no longer capable of making sacrifices, only compromises. What is needed is an "inner will." If the leaders of the East could sense in you the slightest flame, the slightest vital urge for the survival and propagation of liberty, they would understand that you are ready to sacrifice your lives. Then it is they who would immediately lower their guard.
>
> Each time you have shown your resolve—in Berlin, Korea, Cuba—the Soviet leaders have beaten a retreat. The battle is not between you and them, but between you and yourselves.

That is exactly it: the battle is between us and ourselves. That is Christian revolution, which begins when we have revolted against ourselves and enthroned Jesus as Lord. As *The Living Bible* paraphrase puts 2 Corinthians 5:17, "When someone becomes a Christian he becomes a brand new person inside. He is not the same any more. A new life has begun!"

3

The Third Commandment:

GUARDIAN OF HIS REPUTATION

You shall not take the name of the Lord your God in vain,
for the Lord will not leave him unpunished who takes His
name in vain.   (Exodus 20:7)

As we continue these studies I want to be sure that we have clearly in mind that the gospel of God's saving grace through which we come to know Him by faith in Jesus alone and therefore have forgiveness and life, is never a gospel of license. It is a gospel of liberty within the framework of the law of God. We are saved by faith in order that the righteousness of the Law might be fulfilled in us by His Spirit. The great message of the Christian faith is, therefore, that we are free from the Law's condemnation in order that we may be able to fulfill its obligation by the power of Another (capital *A*) within us, that Other who died to bear our condemnation, living to fulfill every demand that the Law could ever make on us. That is the gospel, not some "deeper teaching" (I do not like these phrases like "deeper life" and such). It is the full gospel, and only a clear recognition of that truth, coupled with an experience of it in which we relax and trust Jesus and stop trying to work up some self-conceived idea of how to live the Christian life, will bring us the peace we all seek. We must stop our wrestling, and nestle into the heart of Jesus, finding His adequacy every day in answer to our faith and confession and repentance.

It is only when we find that which is offered to us in God's Word that we can live the normal Christian life. Nobody can ever enjoy Christian living if he is always asking God for mercy and forgiveness and has never learned to praise the Lord for victory. God has not redeemed us to make us crawl and cringe.

He enables us to stand in His will, to have life, and have it more abundantly (John 10:10). No, it is not a gospel of license but of liberty within the framework of God's law.

At the end of a young-people's meeting a group of them came to speak to me, and they were really angry with me. One girl of about twenty-four said to me, "You don't preach the gospel."

"Really?" I said.

"No, for you don't know my Saviour," she replied.

I said, "If that is so, please tell me about Him."

"He is so wonderful," she said. "He forgives me so freely."

"That is lovely," I said. "He must be a wonderful Saviour, but so is mine."

"Oh, no, you don't really know Him," was her reply, so I asked her to explain what she meant.

"Well, I am an awful liar, you know—really a terrible liar. Only last night I was out on a date and I did not want my mother to know where I was, so I told her a lie."

"What did you do about that?" I asked.

"I went into my room, knelt down by the side of my bed and said, 'Sorry, Lord Jesus, that I told that lie. Thank You for the blood that cleanses from all sin and thank You for forgiveness.' And I went to sleep."

"Why, my dear girl," I said, "you are quite right. I don't know your Saviour. And I am sorry to have to tell you that you don't know mine—you do not know the Saviour revealed in God's Word. There is no such thing as a saved liar—you are saved from lying."

Does that help you understand it is not a gospel of license? It is a gospel of liberty within the framework of God's law.

Now we come to the Third Commandment, and this reminder is all the more necessary, for here is one which we can so easily, and yet unconsciously, break. Let us look first at the meaning of it, then how it is broken, and finally how it is kept.

The name of God always is expressive of the character of God, and every title by which He makes Himself known to us speaks of a different aspect of His character. Let me give you some of the names by which He makes Himself known in His Word to indicate the kind of God He is.

First, in Psalms 23:1, "The Lord is my shepherd"; His name there is *Jehovah Rohi*, "the Lord my shepherd," which speaks of the guidance of God.

In Ezekiel 48:35—"The Lord is there," *Jehovah Shammah*, telling of His presence.

In Exodus 17:15—"The Lord is my banner," *Jehovah Nissi*, speaks of the Lord of victory.

In Exodus 31:13—"I am the Lord who sanctifies you," *Jehovah Machaddesh*, the God of holiness.

In Psalms 24:10—"The Lord of hosts," *Jehovah Tsabbaoth*, telling of His authority.

In Jeremiah 23:6—"The Lord our righteousness," *Jehovah Tsidkenu*.

In Genesis 22:14—"The Lord will provide," *Jehovah Jireh*.

Finally, in Judges 6:24—"The Lord is peace," *Jehovah Shalom*.

It would be a study in itself for you to take each one of those names and titles of God in its context and see how wonderfully it opens up a different aspect of His character. From each different title we learn something new about our wonderful Lord. This Commandment tells us that if we take upon our lips His name, we must never deny His character. This is brought out in Isaiah 48:1:

> Hear this, O house of Jacob, who are named Israel
> And who came forth from the loins of Judah,
> Who swear by the name of the Lord
> And invoke the God of Israel,
> But not in truth nor in righteousness.

They were using the name of the Lord, but failing to obey the revelation behind it.

Of course, they had their counterparts in the New Testament. Listen to what the Lord Jesus says in Matthew 7:22, 23:

> Many will say to Me on that day, "Lord, Lord, did we not prophesy in Your name, and in Your name cast out demons, and in Your name perform many miracles?" And then I will declare to them, "I never knew you; DEPART FROM ME, YOU WHO PRACTICE LAWLESSNESS."

You notice that He did not say "two or three" or "a few," but *"many* in that day." What a shock for those who assumed they were all right because they said and did the right thing: spoke of the Lord, witnessed, visited, preached, and so on. It is possible for such a person to be zealous and completely orthodox and fundamental, yet for it never to have occurred to him that he could be anything but a Christian. But the Lord Jesus Himself says, "I never knew you."

That is a shattering revelation of the Lord Jesus. It is not my word, but His. Many, alas, may never have had a vital saving relationship with Him, and are lost. There are people using His name to witness, to do mighty works, but they themselves are unknown to the King. A man uses the name of the Lord in vain when he himself in his life is not true to the revelation of it. "The Lord will not hold him guiltless"—as the King James Version puts it—and that literally translated would read, "The Lord will not hold him clean."

What a searching test that is! The test of being accounted clean before God is the attitude of a man to the name of God. I would think it far better never to mention His name, perhaps never even to have heard it, than constantly to talk of His name and then deny Him with a self-loving life. In other words, my dear friend, the test of life is character. A Christian inevitably is an expression of the character of God, because he is indwelt by His Holy Spirit every moment of the day. He is a guardian of the reputation of the living Lord Jesus.

Just as the moon reflects the light of the sun into the darkness of the night, so the Christian is meant to be a reflector of the light which is Christ *in* him. As he turns his eyes upon Jesus and looks full in His wonderful face, then he catches something of the glow and reality from heaven and reflects His beauty into the darkness of the world. He is the guardian of the reputation of Christ.

The great Charles H. Spurgeon once said, "What is the value of the grace we profess to receive which leaves us exactly the same kind of people as we were before we received it? An unholy life is an evidence of an unchanged heart, and an unchanged heart is an evidence of an unsaved soul."

"Many have said to Me . . . but I say to you, Depart, I never knew you." To assume the name of the Lord is to express in our lives His character, and that is the meaning of this Commandment.

Now how can this command be broken? In three ways: by profanity, by frivolity, by hypocrisy. Let us look at these in more depth.

I trust none of us are guilty of breaking this law by profanity, although we might have been at one time. There are some who, amazing to say, do not believe in God, never speak to Him or go to church, yet who in nearly every sentence use His name in blasphemy and cursing, almost unconsciously. That is demoralizing.

Another way God's name is used in vain is by frivolity. By that is meant using the name of the Lord in jokes, the frivolous use of the name of Jesus in songs, the superficial lighthearted program that so often we put over, the exaggerated account of God's blessing on His work in order to produce funds for future operations. Against all these evidences of a law that is despised, God speaks to us in judgment. It is true to say that a man who has never wilted before the Lord has never begun to worship.

It was the man who, looking up to heaven, caught a vision of God's holiness and cried, "Woe is me, for I am ruined! Because I am a man of unclean lips . . ." (Isaiah 6:5). For five chapters in his prophecy Isaiah had said, "Woe to you . . . ." He was denouncing everyone else until he saw the awesome sight of God's glory, and then he cried, "Woe is *me!*"

It was on the isle of Patmos in the Mediterranean where John the Apostle said, "I heard behind me a loud voice . . . and I turned to see the voice . . . and when I saw Him, I fell at His feet as a dead man" (Revelation 1:10, 12, 17). It was not thrill or excitement, or enthusiasm, but it was sheer fear that gripped him as he met the risen Lord.

You may disagree with me, but personally I do not believe a man ever comes to know God until he is afraid of Him, and has seen something of His majesty, His glory, His power, His greatness, alongside his own insignificance and desperate sin. Then he becomes afraid and trembles at His presence. A man never really works in real power until he has learned to wait in fear and submission before the name of the Lord. That will effectively kill the superficiality which bedevils so many of our Christian programs.

Perhaps the most awful and subtle form in which this law is broken is by hypocrisy: by the man who says "Lord!" but does not keep His Commandments. Jesus said, "And why do you call Me, 'Lord, Lord,' and do not do what I say?" (Luke 6:46). Have you ever found a satisfactory answer to that? I haven't.

It is an unanswerable question.

The hypocrisy of the Church is far worse than the profanity of the street. The blasphemy of the pew is a more insidious form of evil than the blasphemy of the slum. To pray and not to practice, to believe and not to obey, to praise and yet at heart to rebel, is to take the name of the Lord in vain. To come to church, to preach with eloquent lips and fitting words, with correct attitude and everything right, then to go home and break this Commandment is the worst of all. It is usually possible to tell how far a message from the Word of God has got home by the way a congregation leaves church.

I remember having a crusade in Belfast, Northern Ireland, one time, when there were about 9000 people out every night. It was in a huge arena, and I preached from a boxing ring in the center. Special streetcars were running out from the city to bring the crowds. There was great interest and a tremendous moving, and people were saying that revival had come at last. But I was not so sure, and one night after the message I said to my song leader, "Do you mind finishing the service? I am going out." So he took over, and out I went. It was dark and cold, and I stood behind a stone pillar where I could not be seen, and I watched 9000 people go out of that place. You would think they had been to a comedy show! The fellows lit up their cigarettes, put their arms around their girl friends, and chatted about everything under the sun—and I had sought to confront them with the realities of heaven and hell.

Do you see what I mean? How do you leave your church? Is the conversation subdued? Is there an awesomeness of the sense that you have met in the presence of God and He has been dealing with His people? Is your first desire to go straight home with your family and pray together? Is your concern that somehow what you have heard might become part of your life? Or are you busy making a date, arranging to watch a TV program, going out fishing, or whatever?

"You shall not take the name of the Lord your God in vain." When life does not square with profession, and when conduct does not line up with conviction, then a man finds himself guilty.

"Not every one who says to Me, 'Lord, Lord,' will enter the kingdom of heaven; but he who does the will of My Father who is in heaven" (Matthew 7:21). Faith which is not backed by absolute repentance and followed by unqualified obedience is not valid in terms of New Testament salvation.

If we sense the force of this, how may this Commandment be kept? If the Holy Spirit has been speaking to you, what is the answer? It is very thrilling, really. The name of God is expressed perfectly in Jesus. Every aspect of God's character is revealed in Him: "For in Him all the fulness of Deity dwells in bodily form, and in Him you have been made complete . . ." (Colossians 2:9, 10). He lives that He might fulfill His obedience to this law in your life and mine.

"For there is no other name under heaven that has been given among men, by which we must be saved" (Acts 4:12). Of course, there is no other name that can bring redemption, but He can and He has. Go back to those names of God again.

Jehovah Rohi, the Lord is my shepherd—who is that but the Lord Jesus, the Good Shepherd of John 10? Do you submit to His guidance, honestly? When you go to Him concerning a problem, when you don't know which way to turn or what to do, do you ask for His guidance, or do you approach Him with your mind made up, merely wanting Him to OK your decision? Have you not discovered, dear Christian friend, that the Lord Jesus refuses to be your rubber stamp? He will not sign on your dotted line. "The Lord is my shepherd"—He will guide if you submit to His leading.

Jehovah Shammah, the Lord who is there. That speaks of His presence. Do you count on His presence every moment of every day? First thing each morning can you say, "Thank you, Lord Jesus, that You are with me right now. You never leave me or forsake me." Each moment of the day He is there, and He is absolutely adequate for every situation. I can say to you, not only from the Word of God but from my own experience, that I have proved for over forty years that Jesus is adequate. The only right I have to speak to any congregation at any time, anywhere, is because I *know* that Jesus is sufficient.

If you submit to His guidance, if you count on His presence—ah, but there is much more! If you experience His victory: *Jehovah Nissi,* the Lord is my banner, my victory. Are you living in victory, having declared total war on the flesh? Have you realized that you do not have to struggle and fight for victory? When Jesus died, rose, and ascended to heaven and poured His Holy Spirit into your life, He provided for victory in every situation you might experience. I wonder what that situation is, but it is none of my business, and Jesus knows. Yes, He knows about that heartache; He knows about that problem; He knows about the illness or the tragedy in your life; He knows about that defeat with the devastating sense of shame; He knows about that unhappy home. Yes, He knows the whole situation. In fact, He has allowed it all to come into your life to bring you to the point when you stop struggling and begin trusting.

A phrase often used in prayer and praise is a wonderful statement: "The steadfast of mind Thou wilt keep in perfect peace, Because he trusts in Thee" (Isaiah 26:3). Instead of *asking* the Lord Jesus, why not start *thanking* Him for victory? Instead of pleading, "O please, Lord, I am in a tight jam and don't know which way to turn! I am right up against it, going round in circles—please help," rather say to Him, "Lord Jesus, I am right at the end of my rope; I cannot move, for I don't know which way to turn—but thank You; I believe that You are sufficient right now."

Read 2 Chronicles 20 sometime. When Jehoshaphat got himself into real problems through his own compromise, he turned to prayer and sought the Lord. You are safe when you do that. Jehoshaphat said, "Lord, look at this great enemy that comes against me. I don't know what to do, but my eyes are upon You." Would that be true of you in relation to your own life? If you confess "I don't know what to do, but my eyes are upon You," then His answer comes clearly back to you: "Stand still. See the salvation of the Lord with you today, for the battle is not yours but the Lord's." What a relief! The responsibility is on His shoulders! "Set yourselves; see the salvation of the Lord with you this day, and tomorrow go out against them." So when Jehoshaphat had got firmly fixed in his mind that the battle was not his but the Lord's, he picked a choir from the crowd, and they went into battle praising the Lord, rejoicing and thanking Him, and we read, "when the people began to sing and to praise, the Lord sent ambushments against the enemy."

There is tremendous power in praise! When I really begin to praise the Lord with all my heart, even though I am surrounded by foes who are too great for me, but I know my heart is right with Him, therefore I also know that, thanks to His faithfulness, He gives me the victory. That does not mean to say that circumstances alter drastically, but it does mean to say that my attitude toward them does. It means I am proving the adequacy of Christ as I go through life. Peace is not inactivity; it is movement without friction.

Jehovah Machaddesh, the Lord does sanctify, the Lord my holiness. Are you revealing that in your life anew today—His holiness, His purity, His sweetness?

Jehovah Tsabbaoth, the Lord of hosts. Do you really bow to His authority? Have you accepted and unquestionably acknowledged that in every part of your life He is Lord and Sovereign of all? He must be Lord of your bankbook, of your personal home life as well as your business and social life. Is Jesus truly your Lord?

Jehovah Tsidkenu, the Lord our righteousness. Have you rejected your own righteousness and accepted His? "My hope is built on nothing less than Jesus' blood and righteousness" is the only response that saves and blesses.

Jehovah Jireh, the Lord will provide. Do you rest in Him when you face an impossibility, or do you panic and worry? Panic and worry choke the channel through which His Holy Spirit can flow to reach you in your time of need.

Finally, *Jehovah Shalom,* the Lord is peace. When God implants into your heart His Holy Spirit, He implants His name, which is His character. From that moment you become a guardian of His reputation, which can be an almost terrifying responsibility.

So I would ask, What are you doing with that name? What a tragedy to find that somewhere along the line you may have deceived yourself. How do you think that happens? It is because we have a false conception of the doctrine of eternal security. Of course I believe in the eternal security of the believer, but are we quite sure what we mean by that term *believer?* There is such a danger of basing our salvation on mere formula, on statements that we take out of context in the Bible, such as "Believe in the Lord Jesus, and you shall be saved . . ." (Acts 16:31). A verse like that cannot be given by itself; it must be in its context.

James says in 2:19 of his letter, "You believe that God is one. You do well; the demons also believe, and shudder." This last word actually means "his hair stands on end"! Yes indeed, well may Charles Wesley write,

> Jesus! the Name high over all,
> In hell, or earth, or sky;
> Angels and men before it fall,
> And devils fear and fly.

I want to say to you in Jesus' name that when you and I go out into daily life with such a vital relationship with Him, that same thing can happen, as through us the name of Jesus can rebuke the power of the enemy.

You see, because one can say "I believe in the Lord Jesus," that does not say he is a believer. Read carefully:

> If we say that we have fellowship with Him, and yet walk in the darkness, we lie and do not practice the truth; but if we walk in the light as He Himself is in the light, we have fellowship with one another, and the blood of Jesus His Son cleanses us from all sin . . . . If we say that we have not sinned, we make Him a liar, and His word is not in us.
>
> 1 John 1:6, 7, 10

> The one who says, "I have come to know Him," and does not keep His commandments, is a liar, and the truth is not in him; but whoever keeps His word, in him the love of God has truly been perfected.
>
> 1 John 2:4, 5

That is a shattering exposure of the disaster of the preaching of "easy believism." However much a person may say he believes in Christ, if the habitual practice of his life is sinful, then he is taking the name of the Lord in vain.

Now if you think I am preaching sinless perfection, let me tell you I am not. I am preaching sinful corruption, and can tell you that the only good thing about Alan Redpath or anybody else is the Lord Jesus Christ. All the rest is complete failure. But, thank God, all that has been dealt with at the cross. That is not sinless perfection, for the only sinlessly perfect One is Jesus Himself, and because He indwells His people, He gives them the power to fulfill His word and obey His commands.

What are we doing today with the name of the Lord? The Holy Spirit has been talking and exposing the breakdown and failure and inconsistency in our lives. But that is what we are, and if the devil points a finger at us, we can thank the Lord that He has told us about this long ago, and anything Satan says is not nearly so bad, as the Lord has shown to us in His Word. How we thank Him that this is all He expects, for that is what we are in ourselves. How we need to ask Him to clothe us with His loveliness, that we might exalt His name, be true guardians of His reputation, and never grieve Him by taking His name in vain.

4
The Fourth Commandment:
WORSHIP AND WORK

Remember the sabbath day, to keep it holy. Six days you shall labor and do all your work, but the seventh day is a sabbath of the Lord your God; in it you shall not do any work, you or your son or your daughter, your male servant or your female servant or your cattle or your sojourner who stays with you. For in six days the Lord made the heavens and the earth, the sea and all that is in them, and rested on the seventh day; therefore the Lord blessed the sabbath day and made it holy. (Exodus 20:8–11)

Now consider with me the implication of this command as it stands. It has to do with what concerns every one of us, and that is both work and rest. These are essential for life, and are God's will for everybody: work and worship. Work in the will of God is part of worship. Worship, meditation, praise are the highest work of which anybody is capable. A man who does not work is unfit for worship. The man who never worships is incapable of work. Work and worship are God's intention for every human being. A man should be both a worker and a worshiper—which reminds me of a story told of the late Bishop Taylor-Smith, who, when he visited homes or hotels and met the staff, would greet them by saying, "Make your work your worship, and worship while you work."

The Sabbath day was never intended to be a day of gloom or restriction, but a day of gladness to think upon God, to cease from work, and to worship with a view to greater consecration for each day's task. Obedience to this Commandment creates power to obey the others. The person who maintains a right balance in life between work and worship has made a great discovery.

Now please notice that the Bible does not suggest a five-day week: "Six days you shall labor and do all your work." And, within the limited scope of this command, it holds true today When the Sabbath day of rest becomes the day of recreation instead of the day of worship, it never achieves its purpose. The problem in the Church today is that the Lord's day has become the Lord's *half* day. People attend the morning worship or education hour and then spend the rest of the day in various recreational activities. I wonder who once thought up the idea that the pastor preaches to the saints in the morning and sinners in the evening? I gave that up long ago for the simple reason that the people who came to the evening service were not the sinners, if I may use such a derogatory term, but they were the saints who backed up the pastor, who wanted to show him that they would support him, and came to do so at the evening service. Far more sinners are to be found at the morning service than at the evening. But of course, in so many instances, the story is "as it was in the beginning, is now, and ever shall be—nothing changes in our church, so we carry on doing the same thing as ever." It is a great problem in the Church today that this rest day, the day of worship, has been turned into a day of recreation.

But this Commandment has a much wider and deeper meaning than this. It contains the revelation of God's plan of redemption right from Genesis to Revelation.

Therefore I want to speak to you first about the rest of creation. The Lord says here, "Remember the sabbath day." That statement reverts to Genesis 1, the story of God's creation, or better, His restoration of a previous disaster. Then it is written, "Thus the heavens and the earth were completed, and all their hosts. And by the seventh day God completed His work which He had done; and He rested on the seventh day from all His work which He had done" (Genesis 2:1, 2).

The Lord did not rest because He was weary; He rested because He was satisfied, as He saw that all He had performed was very good. On the sixth day God's greatest work of creation was to make man in His own image, after His likeness. Man therefore, who had nothing to do with God's creative activity, was created on the sixth day, and could enter with God into the rest of satisfaction on the seventh day, and enjoy it.

I want you to understand that, because you will see the importance of it later on. The man God created had nothing to do in helping Him create anything. God made it all—all this glorious universe and the beautiful earth we inhabit—and on the seventh day with sheer satisfaction He looked around and enjoyed it. With Him was the man created in His own image, who at his first waking, conscious moments, as it were, was to enter in with His Creator to enjoy His creation with Him.

Alas, that that rest of creation did not last! It was ruined by sin, and man's relationship with God was ruined too. That rest of satisfaction was quickly ended.

Turning to the New Testament we find out what is said there about the Sabbath day and how the Lord Jesus regarded it. Some people suggest He dispensed with it, but that is not so.

> At that time Jesus went on the Sabbath through the grainfields, and His disciples became hungry and began to pick the heads of grain and eat. But when the Pharisees saw it, they said to Him, "Behold, Your disciples do what is not lawful to do on a Sabbath."
>
> But He said to them, "Have you not read what David did, when he became hungry, he and his companions; how he entered the house of God, and they ate the consecrated bread, which was not lawful for him to eat, nor for those with him, but for the priests alone? Or have you not read in the Law, that on the Sabbath the priests in the temple break the Sabbath, and are innocent? But I say to you, that something greater than the temple is here. But if you had known what this means, 'I DESIRE COMPASSION, AND NOT A SACRIFICE,' you would not have condemned the innocent. For the Son of Man is Lord of the Sabbath."
>
> Matthew 12:1–8

Do we understand the implications of those verses? As Jesus went for a walk on a Sabbath day with His disciples they were exercising their privilege of plucking and eating grain in the fields, which was quite legal. Deuteronomy 23:25 gave them that authority under the Law, that when they went into their neighbor's field they were entitled to pluck the grain, but not to put in the sickle. In other words, sample and taste the grain, but do not reap or harvest it. The disciples therefore were doing what they were entitled to do. But the Pharisees (they are always on the watch!) were on the same walk with one avowed purpose, to trip up our Lord and to find some inconsistency in His life and in the disciples'. This act of theirs seemed to the Pharisees absolutely unlawful, for it involved breaking the Sabbath. Interpreted by them, plucking grain was reaping, and this meant work, which the Commandment forbids.

How did our Lord deal with them? His first reply recalls the incident of David and the shewbread. The story is in 1 Samuel 21. David was running away from Saul, and in an emergency went to the house of the priest, and though God's law restricted the shewbread for the use of the priests (Leviticus 24:9), the extreme need of David and the emergency of the situation overruled that regulation, a fact which the Pharisees themselves accepted. It is evident also from Matthew 12:5 that the law of Sabbath rest was not absolute, for the priests were required by that very law to work on the Sabbath and serve the temple (Numbers 28:9, 10).

The Lord's argument quite clearly is that if the priests are guiltless in working on the Sabbath to further the interests of the temple worship, how much more are His disciples guiltless in using the Sabbath for the work of Christ, who is the reality to which the temple pointed! He summed it all up when He said (*see* Matthew 12:6, 7), "If only you understood, you people who are so particular about detail, that God requires mercy and not sacrifice, the heart and not the external; for the Son of Man is Lord of the Sabbath, and those who use the Sabbath day in My interest are using it rightly." The Sabbath is made for man, and not man for the Sabbath (*see* Mark 2:27). It is not a day of restriction but a day of rejoicing.

There is a deeper meaning in the New Testament than that. It speaks not only of the rest of creation but of reconciliation. The death of the Lord Jesus on the cross showed the whole significance of this great day. Apparently without any instruction given in the Word of God, at the moment the Christian era began the Sabbath day was changed from the seventh day to the first. Why? God had rested in creation, and man with Him. That rest was shaken, disturbed and destroyed by sin. The one sacrifice of Calvary completed a finished work, and that relationship is restored immediately in reconciliation, and the death of Jesus reestablished that relationship. A perfect work of salvation was accomplished when the Lord Jesus rose on the first day of the week and then entered into rest.

God, who rested in creation, now rests in reconciliation. The man who had nothing whatever to do with the work of creation but rested to enjoy it, now has nothing to do with the work of reconciliation but rests on the first day to enjoy it. Of course that is the answer to the Seventh-day Adventist. When Jesus died and rose on the first day of the week, the empty tomb demonstrated God's satisfaction with the finished work of redemption, and God and man are reconciled. God's relationship with man is restored to what it was originally at the day of man's creation. God the Creator could smile upon His work and enjoy it, and share the enjoyment with the man He created. Now God the Father can smile in satisfaction upon His Son in the work of regeneration, redemption, and reconciliation, and invite those who have nothing at all to do with it to enter into it all, and enjoy it.

> My Saviour, Thou hast offered rest,
>   O grant it then to me—
> The rest of ceasing from myself
>   To find my all in Thee.
>
> In Thy strong hand I lay me down,
>   So shall the work be done;
> For who can work so wondrously
>   As the Almighty One?
>   ELIZA H. HAMILTON

Under Law men worked toward rest—the Sabbath day was the seventh day—and by the Law is the knowledge of sin. God's original intention at creation was for men to enter into rest and then go to work. But sin ruined that, and the teaching of the Old Testament should have shown man that no longer did he rest and work, but he had been made to work and then rest. Now, in the New Testament, the situation is as before— the believer enters into rest, and from that rest goes out to work: "There remains therefore a Sabbath rest for the people of God. For the one who has entered His rest has himself also rested from his works, as God did from His" (Hebrews 4:9, 10).

Now he is reconciled to God: "But when the kindness of God our Savior and His love for mankind appeared, He saved us, not on the basis of deeds which we have done in righteousness, but according to His mercy, by the washing of regeneration and renewing by the Holy Spirit, whom He poured out upon us richly through Jesus Christ our Savior" (Titus 3:4–6). By faith he can enter into Christ's perfect work, enter into that rest and enjoy it with the Lord, and from that rest go out and serve.

This is significant for two reasons, first in relation to this command: "Remember the sabbath day, to keep it holy." That is why we should keep it holy and set it apart for worship, that from that rest we might serve. Of course, every day we celebrate the resurrection of the Lord Jesus. Every day the risen Lord indwells our hearts and lives. But somehow there is something very special about the Lord's day, the first day of the week, a day when we can remember what He has done for us, and worship.

Of course, we again are faced with the same problem the disciples faced, and with which the Lord dealt in Matthew 12. Is a Sunday a day of rest for the minister or Christian worker? I should say not. Surely the important thing—remembering that the Lord does not concern Himself with external details but with internal reality—is maintaining the balance in life between rest and work, between work and worship.

There is an illustration of that principle in Mark 3:13–15: "And He went up to the mountain and summoned those whom He Himself wanted, and they came to Him. And He appointed twelve, that they might be with Him, and that He might send them out to preach, and to have authority to cast out the demons."

These twelve men were to perpetuate the ministry of the Kingdom of God on earth, and they were to do it by being in *with* Him, called *by* Him, and then going out *for* Him. The man who is in with Jesus is a disciple; the one who goes out for Him is an apostle, a "sent one." These twelve men were to live a life of discipleship and apostleship, to be with Him and out for Him.

To get down to this question of rest and work: If you were asked how your Christian life is getting along, your answer might well be, "It is a bit up and down. On Sunday night I am on cloud nine, but on Monday morning I'm often not fit to live with."

The Lord never intended His people to be up and down, but

He does intend them to be in and out! In for worship, out for work. In for orders, out in obedience. In for surrender, out for service.

This is the area perhaps of the hardest battle of all in Christian living, and often it is lost. If the child of God is always *in* for worship he gets spiritual indigestion. If he is always *out* in work he becomes spiritually ineffective, and we are all in danger of that. Who has not suffered either a nervous breakdown, a total collapse, or some physical problem because he is always doing and never being, always out and never in? Beware of the barrenness of a busy life which majors in work and minors in worship.

Look at the twelve disciples: there was not a Ph.D. among them! There were very few with any education. They were an ignorant lot of nobodies, but they were those whom Jesus desired. Mind you, He did not set any prejudice against education, for ultimately Paul was a disciple. But this little crowd of precious nobodies were those whom He wanted. They were absolutely raw, and before they went out for Him they had to be in with Him. As you read their names you cannot fail to be impressed by what an unlikely crew they were! Not one of them would have stood a chance with any pulpit vacancy committee or candidate department of a missionary society today! There are Simon Peter and John, side by side. If Peter were living in the United States, his favorite words would be *rush—instant—let's go—action!*

Then John, the dreamer, leaning on Jesus' breast. Put those two men together on a mission station and in less than no time there is a casualty through incompatibility of temperament.

Next is Matthew, who sold himself to the Roman government to collect taxes for it. Alongside him is Simon the Canaanite, a Zealot, who would be all for riots and revolution to overthrow the system. Put those two side by side and you have a fight on your hands.

But, you see, Jesus called them that they might be with Him. I am stressing this because of the vital importance of the whole emphasis of this Commandment. You cannot possibly observe the Lord's day inactively as a Christian worker, but for seven days a week there must be the balance between work and worship.

I learned that lesson the hard way eventually, because God

had to lay me aside to teach me some things. I would not have missed a period of serious illness for anything, because the Lord Jesus has been much more precious to me since then, much more real. As a pastor I had made the colossal error of substituting work for worship, and God caught up with me and laid me on my back to teach me a lesson. I think I have learned that lesson and share with you one sentence which might be the key to it: Never attempt more work for God than you can cover in believing prayer. If you do, you will find yourself on your own. You can expect God's blessing only on that which you have covered in His presence in believing, earnest, prevailing prayer. I believe that is the principle and the answer.

Moses, in Exodus 33, was harassed by a great multitude of people for whose leadership he was responsible, about three million of them. He did not say, "Lord, please get rid of them. I cannot cope with their grouses any longer. I've had enough!" No indeed, but this is what he said: "I pray Thee, show me Thy glory!" (verse 18).

Is there any glory around in your church? Is there any glory around in your home and in your own life? "I pray you, Lord, break through the pressures and everything that seems to hem me in, and just shine into my heart with Your glory from heaven." That is all you need. The result for Moses was that God spoke with him as a man speaks face to face with his friend. And that can be your experience too.

Whether a man is responsible for the pastoral care of a few or a thousand, every person to whom he speaks, every work, class, or fellowship, has a right to see a man who speaks to God face to face as one speaks with his friend.

Has the glory been getting somewhat tarnished lately and growing dim? Has the interview with Jesus face to face never been real—or not real for a long time? Perhaps pressures, tensions, and many other things have taken over, and you have failed in your obedience to this command, to retain the balance between rest and work, between worship and service. Remember the Lord's day and the biblical significance. Remember that it means that God in His creation entered into rest and made man in His image to share it with Him and enjoy it all. Remember, in our redemption He has done precisely the same thing, but He wants *friends* who share with Him the joy of His risen life. Sonship with God depends upon faith. Friendship with God depends upon obedience. Therefore the big question is whether He can depend upon our total obedience all the time.

This Commandment speaks of another thing too: not only of the Sabbath day, but—by implication—of the fact that there remains a rest for the people of God, the rest of regeneration. I wonder if you have entered into it. The Lord Jesus said, "Come to Me, all who are weary and heavy-laden, and I will give you rest. Take My yoke upon you, and learn from Me, for I am gentle and humble in heart; and YOU SHALL FIND REST FOR YOUR SOULS. For My yoke is easy, and My load is light" (Matthew 11:28–30).

The moment a person is born again he enters in by faith to the rest of a finished work. But have you ever entered into that rest that He promises when you take His yoke and find rest to your soul? It does not mean that the Christian is a lazy person and does nothing. Oh, no! Listen to Paul's language in Colossians 1:29: ". . . I labor, striving according to His power, which mightily works within me." Yet Paul had entered into that rest in Christ.

The rest of which I speak means movement without friction, like an eight-cylinder car rolling along the road smoothly with everything working properly, the whole thing without friction. Movement without friction, that is rest. "I labor . . . according to His power, which mightily works within me"—that is the secret of the exchanged life.

"Those who wait for the Lord will gain new strength," said Isaiah (40:31), and that literally means they exchange their strength for His. Paul knew it when the Lord said to him, "My grace is sufficient for you, for power is perfected in weakness," so that he was able to add, "for when I am weak, then I am strong" (2 Corinthians 12:9, 10).

To rest in Jesus like that is what this Commandment is all about, to learn the balance between rest and worship, and then to go out to work, not in one's own strength, but in His, knowing that He gives grace for everything that is in His will.

This can be said so easily, but to practice it is another matter. I don't mind telling that there are many days when at the end of them I find myself at the end of my rope. If anyone knows what exhaustion is, I do; but I do know always what it is to enjoy the adequacy of His grace for everything that is in His will. So you who are busy in Christian life and activity may also prove that His grace is sufficient. But if you are attempting to do something, and find yourself at wit's end because you are carrying a burden far too great, it may well be that you are attempting to do something that is not the will of God for you.

We have considered the rest of creation, the rest of reconciliation, the rest of regeneration, and now consider one further aspect: "Blessed are the dead who die in the Lord from now on! 'Yes,' says the Spirit, 'that they may rest from their labors, for their deeds follow with them' " (Revelation 14:13).

In creation God worked from the evening to the morning, as recorded in the Book of Genesis, chapter 1: "And there was evening and there was morning, one day" (verse 5); "And there was evening and there was morning, a second day" (verse 8), and so on. He works now from the gloom of the cross, the midnight of Calvary, to a morning of realization. We work from the morning to the evening, but there is coming a day when we shall enter into the rest of realization. Let these wonderful words sink into your soul:

> These are the ones who come out of the great tribulation, and they have washed their robes and made them white in the blood of the Lamb. For this reason, they are before the throne of God; and they serve Him day and night in His temple; and He who sits on the throne shall spread His tabernacle over them. They shall hunger no more, neither thirst any more; neither shall the sun beat down on them, nor any heat; for the Lamb in the center of the throne shall be their shepherd, and shall guide them to springs of the water of life; and God shall wipe every tear from their eyes.
>
> Revelation 7:14–17

That is the rest of realization when His people serve Him day and night in His temple.

Do you ever think about heaven? I suppose as we get older we are inclined to wonder about the sort of mansion God has for us in Glory. I have no idea, but I tell you one thing I do know, that in whatever home He has for me in heaven there will be missing one room in which I have spent a great deal of time down here—and that is a bedroom! We will serve Him day and night in His temple. The nature which we shall wear in Glory—redeemed, ransomed, restored, forgiven, the nature of the risen Christ—never wearies or tires, but rests always in eternal activity in serving Him forever.

Therefore, "remember the sabbath day, to keep it holy," because of God's rest in reconciliation which we can enjoy now, the rest of regeneration into which we may enter now, and the rest of realization which we will enjoy perfectly one day with Him in Glory.

5

The Fifth Commandment:

PRESERVE OUR HOMES

Honor your father and your mother, that your days may be prolonged in the land which the Lord your God gives you. (Exodus 20:12)

The Ten Commandments are not merely from an Old Testament dispensation, they are the blueprint for all happiness. Obedience to them always brings harmony with the purpose of God and in relation to other people too, for holiness and happiness are inseparable.

The Law was first of all given to Israel on the basis of redemption. In Exodus 20:2 the Lord said, "I am the Lord your God, who brought you out of the land of Egypt, out of the house of slavery." This was the basis of all further relationships with the Redeemer. But no sooner had the Law been given than it was broken, and the people stood condemned and proved guilty: "Now we know that whatever the Law says, it speaks to those who are under the Law, that every mouth may be closed, and all the world may become accountable to God" (Romans 3:19).

The Law has opened our eyes and shut our mouths, and left us without excuse. But the great revelation of New Testament truth, the gospel, comes shining right through: "For Christ is the end [or fulfillment] of the law for righteousness to everyone who believes" (Romans 10:4).

He is the fulfillment of the Law, our Deliverer. We can come to Him through faith in Him alone, and then He is made unto us righteousness. Theologically, that is imputed righteousness—which means our relationship with God is established. That is, of course, only the beginning.

There is therefore now no condemnation for those who are in Christ Jesus. For the law of the Spirit of life in Christ Jesus has set you free from the law of sin and of death. For what the Law could not do, weak as it was through the flesh, God did: sending His own Son in the likeness of sinful flesh and as an offering for sin, He condemned sin in the flesh, in order that the requirement of the Law might be fulfilled in us [not *by* us], who do not walk according to the flesh, but according to the Spirit.

Romans 8:1–4

So He imparts life, and that is imparted righteousness, which means our relationship with God may be developed. That life is imparted not to excuse our failures, but to enable us not to fail. In Jesus, ". . . neither is circumcision anything, nor uncircumcision, but a new creation" (Galatians 6:15), because now ". . . the love of God has been poured out within our hearts through the Holy Spirit who was given to us" (Romans 5:5).

My obedience therefore is not legal, but inspired by love and empowered by God's Holy Spirit. Does New Testament grace allow a lower standard than Old Testament law? God forbid. It will be seen in the second half of the Decalogue that this is not so. Indeed, the standard under grace is higher.

The tragic thing in my mind is that liberal theologians are often far more concerned with ethics than we evangelicals. There is a tremendous need for a display of ethical Christian living on the part of those who believe the Bible. It is an absolute scandal that there is civil war in the evangelical church when society is in the mess that it is, when Christian brethren fall out among themselves over minor doctrinal matters while two-thirds of the earth's population are rushing to a Christless eternity. What a tragic thing that is in evangelical circles.

Now let us apply all this to the Fifth Commandment. The first four have to do with our relationship to God, and the remainder with our relationship to other people. I think it is very significant that this particular command appears where it does. The family was God's first institution, and society is the family projected and amplified. It is in the home that each of us is prepared and trained to take his place of responsibility, and therefore the importance of the home cannot possibly be over-estimated.

If you ask a minister in Northern Ireland how many members he has, he will tell you he has so many families in his church. He estimates the size of his church by the number of families, and that is a pretty good estimate. It is the family that makes the church and creates society. Everything centers upon the family, and you and I know only too well that tremendous forces are at work today to cause disintegration of the home and rob it of its character. Much of the time of parents and children is spent away from home, not only at work, but in the movies, at parties, clubs, and so on. Often when the family is at home together the TV does all the talking. Home to many people is no more than a last resort when there is nothing else to do, regarding it as a restaurant or a dormitory.

Now this command strikes at the very root of home life, and it is not confined to children, because there is something that refers to all the family. Let us therefore look at this Commandment as it stands: "Honor your father and your mother." The word *honor* means "reverence": *Reverence* your father and your mother. The parent is regarded as being in the place of God to the child. The supreme facts concerning God will be impressed upon the child as he sees them in his parents; and what God is to the adult, the parent is to the child—lawgiver, lover, provider, guide, and so on. What the Lord is to us, we are to the children. A child who responds to that relationship will find it far easier to respond to the claims of the Lord Jesus Christ. Happy is the child who learns from honoring his parents to hallow the name of God; and happy are the parents who so hallow the name of Jesus that it is easy for the children to honor them.

The reason why the children of some Christian, churchgoing families sometimes rebel against the faith of their parents can often be traced to the fact that they see their parents attending church on a Sunday, but during the remainder of the week their time is occupied solely by business, pleasure, the social round, the home, themselves, and there is no connection between the observance of the Sunday church attendance and the rest of life. The young person quite justifiably comes to the conclusion that the Christian faith is just a fake, a pretense without reality, and throws it over. He will continue to live like this, to the deep distress of his parents, until the Lord meets him in a personal encounter and brings him under the convicting, converting power of the Holy Spirit. May parents attend this warning and examine their lives to see they are not proving to be stumbling blocks to their children, instead of stepping-stones to lead them to the Saviour.

However, this word *honor* is not for children only. To honor means much more than to obey. Obedience is included, but the time for a child to obey his parent ceases. The time for him to honor his parents never ceases. To a boy or girl who is not yet of an age to plan or make his decisions, honoring parents includes glad, happy obedience. If you think about it, the very nature of an immature child demands that this should be so. The child is called upon to obey those he loves. When the time comes for him to make his own decisions, he is never exempt from honoring his parents. That honoring will be revealed in love and kindness and devotion in declining years. Where obedience has been given, honoring never fails, and the older a son or daughter becomes, the more he begins to appreciate the care of those early years, and the more eager he is to repay that care with love for his parents. Oh, how happy are the parents who, in the eventide of life, are honored by their family and by children who have come to see how much they owe to their mother's prayers and their father's guidance!

The promise of long life in this Commandment is given to a nation marching toward a land of promise, but it is nevertheless true that obedience to this law results in habit and character which tend to lengthen life, and disobedience can result in the reverse. Obedience to earthly parents makes obedience to the Lord much easier. What a challenge that is to us who are parents! If we would be honored by our family, we must be honorable. The surest way for us to secure the honor of our children is for us to honor the Lord in our homes. If the parent neglects to maintain a time in the daily program for Bible reading and prayer with the family, when together they make their needs and requests known to the Lord, and praise Him for all His many answers, the result will be that instead of a united family there will be angry words, short tempers, and the awful display of an unlimited source of the self-life on the part of both parents and children. "The family that prays together stays together" is not only an easy slogan to remember, it is also a true one.

When children see from an early age that the Word of God means much to their parents, when they realize that the Lord to whom their parents pray not only hears but answers, it will not be hard for such young people to come early to trust, honor, and love the wonderful God who means so much to Mom and Dad. No matter how young a child may be, he has an uncanny knack of being able to distinguish reality from sham, and in no area of life is this more true than in the spiritual. May the Lord save any of us from acting a lie before our children and by so doing maybe leading them into a period of Christ-rejection because we have failed to reveal His preciousness and reality and love to those who have been entrusted to our care.

That is the Commandment as it stands. Now see its interpretation in the New Testament. The Lord Jesus emphasized it constantly by His teaching and example, as is seen in many passages.

> Then some Pharisees and scribes came to Jesus from Jerusalem, saying, "Why do Your disciples transgress the tradition of the elders?" . . . And He answered and said to them, "And why do you yourselves transgress the commandment of God for the sake of your tradition? For God said, 'HONOR YOUR FATHER AND MOTHER,' and 'HE WHO SPEAKS EVIL OF FATHER OR MOTHER, LET HIM BE PUT TO DEATH.' But you say, 'Whoever shall say to his father or mother "Anything of mine you might have been helped by has been given to God," he is not to honor his father or his mother.' And thus you invalidated the word of God for the sake of your tradition."
>
> Matthew 15:1–6.

See how Jesus uses this command to expose an abuse of it at that time. The tradition was that a son might escape responsibility to his parents by saying that what he would have given them was dedicated to God. But Jesus made it absolutely clear that the duty to parents can never be violated in interest to duty to God.

Now that is tremendously important. There are some people who have longed to get to the mission field but who never get there, because they know that their duty is to stay at home with parents who have no other means of support or care but for that son or daughter whose heart aches to serve the Lord overseas. But they know their place is at home and that their duty to God can never violate their duty to their parents. Do we remember that at home, I wonder? Nothing should be given to God which means neglect of duty to our homes, for to do that is to break God's law.

It is important for husbands to realize that time must be given for the family, that it is not superspiritual to be working so hard on committees, church boards, and so on, that one's own children are neglected or tacked onto a busy schedule with the air of "this is the last straw that breaks the camel's back!" Mothers should not fill up their daytime hours to such a degree that they neglect the home, allow the children to come back all the time to an empty home, and have no time to chat and share with the family. So often teenagers are in a sharing mood at the most awkward times, just when dinner is ready to be served up, or the cake is all set to be put into the oven—but all must be left in order to deal with the immediate problem, because an opportunity lost may never be reclaimed. Your teenager may think either that you have no time for him, or that you cannot cope with his particular problems.

Children—and teenagers in particular—must see to it that their activities (especially their Christian activities) do not take them away so much from home that they neglect their share of helping Mom and Dad. So many Christian young people feel that to say "I'm off to my meeting" is a carte blanche to let them off all other chores and responsibilities. "Meetingitis" is a serious complaint that can sever families, stunt meaningful family relationships, and engender a lack of love and caring toward the most precious unit in the world, one's own immediate family. So take care that a so-called activity in the name of the Lord is not merely a cover-up for disinclination to shoulder some responsibilities that are normally part and parcel of "belonging." A testimony to Christ, particularly if a young person is the only Christian in that home, is best given by being helpful and loving, rather than by dashing out night after night to various meetings, thereby neglecting parents and other family members who long perhaps to see how the grace and love of the Lord operates through a life yielded to Him.

This is emphasized again in Ephesians 6:1–4:

> Children, obey your parents in the Lord, for this is right. HONOR YOUR FATHER AND MOTHER (which is the first commandment with a promise), THAT IT MAY BE WELL WITH YOU, AND THAT YOU MAY LIVE LONG ON THE EARTH. And, fathers, do not provoke your children to anger; but bring them up in the discipline and instruction of the Lord.

Here is expressed the lovely atmosphere of a Christian home. You observe that the image of the home in the New Testament centers around the father: "Father, don't nag or irritate your children." The leadership in the home is given to the father, but today so many fathers shirk that in the interest of business, and leave their wives to hold the reins and shoulder the responsibility. It is not right when the image of the home to the children is conveyed to them in terms only of mother. It is the father who is the head of the house, and the father who has the responsibility for caring for his children. I believe that many of our young people have gone off the rails and left home simply because they have never known a father's care, his love and discipline. This is desperately needed, because young children as well as teenagers need to have the security of certain limitations in their behavior, for this shows the caring attitude of the parents. Complete freedom and self-expression (so loved by many educationalists in the past, who are now beginning to see the fruit of these attitudes in lawlessness), given to a child who does not know how to handle them, rather than increasing his joy, gives him a sense of frustration, with the lurking fear that his parents really do not care about him too much. If this continues through the early years, by the time that child is a late teenager, he is off to find folk who *will* care. And alas there are all too many among the false cults as well as among the drug-pushers who, in their own ways, seek to show how much they care, often to the destruction of body and soul.

Needless to say, there are occasions when the father for business and professional reasons has to be away from home for long periods, and on these occasions the mother has to assume a double role. The Lord surely endues such women with special wisdom during such a period, until the man of the house returns and can resume his rightful responsibilities.

Paul says, "Fathers, do not provoke your children, don't nag or irritate them." To me this places the whole responsibility of

Christian education on the parents. I refuse to delegate the onus of sex education to the unconverted schoolteacher. It is the duty of father or mother in the training of their children to educate them in the things that God would have them know, in the right way. For some parents a Christian school is the answer, but whether the school is Christian or not, parents cannot delegate to others—be they the Christian Education department or any school—their responsibility for training their own children.

Too often non-Christian parents (and, alas, some who are believers) turn their children loose, so they spend their time in the movies or in getting into endless trouble. I read that a recent committee on child welfare reported that in 250 films shown on TV there were 97 cases or murder, 51 of adultery, 19 seductions, 22 abductions, 45 suicides, 176 deaths, 25 prostitutes, 35 drunkards. The censorship board sought to eliminate from 780 pictures 1811 cases of assault with intent to kill, 231 cases of hanging, 757 immoral attacks on women, and 929 scenes of nudity. No wonder that the average age of a criminal is about twelve, when children are allowed to look at the TV all the time unchecked, and spend far more time with that than with their family and parents in helpful discussion of some of the things portrayed on the screen and in family sharing. No wonder civilization is in trouble.

The Lord Jesus emphasized this command by His example as He passed through His childhood, and at the age of twelve He was brought by Mary and Joseph to the temple. What a lovely picture we have of a mother's care in Luke 2:48, 49:

> And when they saw Him, they were astonished; and His mother said to Him, "Son, why have You treated us this way? Behold, Your father and I have been anxiously looking for You." And He said to them, "Why is it that you were looking for Me? Did you not know that I had to be in My Father's house?"

Mary was anxious and worried, but there was no rebuke in Jesus' reply. Surely she should know that only the affairs of His heavenly Father would keep Him. These are the first recorded words of our Lord, and in the King James Version of the Bible there is an imperative *must* (rendered "had to be" in the New

American Standard Bible): "I *must* be in My Father's house and about His business." I have written in the margin of my Bible, "O God, may my chidren relate their lives to You by the *must* of complete surrender!"

This little story ends with this statement: "He went down with them . . . and He continued in subjection to them" (Luke 2:51). Yes, He was obedient to His parents. For our dear Lord the years of obedience ultimately ceased, but the years of honor never did. Amid the darkness of Calvary, while on the cross, He planned for His mother, commending her to the care of a loving disciple (John 19:26). Yes, in all this He left us an example that we should follow in His steps. How this law was fulfilled in the life of our Lord Jesus!

But how is this Commandment fulfilled in the life of the child of God today? Turn to two passages which will help, though they may seem to be contradictory:

> Do not think that I came to bring peace on the earth; I did not come to bring peace, but a sword. For I came to SET A MAN AGAINST HIS FATHER, AND A DAUGHTER AGAINST HER MOTHER, AND A DAUGHTER-IN-LAW AGAINST HER MOTHER-IN-LAW; and A MAN'S ENEMIES WILL BE THE MEMBERS OF HIS HOUSEHOLD. He who loves father or mother more than Me is not worthy of Me; and he who loves son or daughter more than Me is not worthy of Me. And he who does not take his cross and follow after Me is not worthy of Me.
>
> Matthew 10:34–38

> If anyone comes to Me, and does not hate his own father and mother and wife and children and brothers and sisters, yes, and even his own life, he cannot be My disciple.
>
> Luke 14:26

That sounds like a contradiction, but it isn't. Jesus did not come to bring peace but to start a war, and He comes to drive a sword through every peace that is not based on a vital personal relationship with Himself. He is Lord of every relationship. He is the only one who can make a home, and He is the only one who has the right to break into it. The only secure home and family is the one at which Jesus is the center, and in which He

is Lord. Duty to God, I have already said, must never conflict
with duty to parents, but love to God will always come first.
That is the distinction. When love comes first in a home there is
surely a preview of heaven, for father and mother love each
other all the more when they have children who love Jesus more
than them, and put His will first; and children love their parents all the more when they see Mom and Dad putting Christ
first. When Jesus is at the center, what a happy home that is! If
boys or girls seek to fulfill this law, they do it most of all by
crowning Jesus as Lord of their life, and if parents would fulfill
their responsibility to this command, they would gladly give
their children to the service of the Lord Jesus.

A word to parents: Have you ever prayed "Lord, please help
Yourself to at least one of our family, and take him or her to
serve you in the uttermost parts of the earth"? If He takes you
up on that and finally it comes to the valedictory service when
you say good-bye to your precious son or daughter whom you
probably will not see for four or five years, I tell you there will
be a twinkle in one eye and a tear in the other! Yes, you are so
thrilled because your child is telling the whole Church, telling
the Lord, and telling the devil, that the thing that matters most
to him or her is the will of God; so for you there is a twinkle of
joy accompanied by a very natural and human tear.

Have you ever prayed like that? There are many parents who
are thoroughly satisfied if their children go into the family
business and live near at hand so that the grandchildren can be
around all the time. That is lovely, and it may be the will of
God, but also it may *not* be—and the Lord has a right to break
into your home and help Himself.

Some missionary friends of mine had seven children, and
when I saw the father recently he told me that never since they
were married had the whole family been together. But all seven
children are serving the Lord, scattered in many parts of the
world under different missions. The Lord had been free to help
Himself to those children.

Now let me be careful to say it is no greater thing to serve the
Lord on the foreign "fields" than it is to tap a typewriter in the
homeland if you are in the will of God. That is what matters
most. But do let us recognize the absolute authority and right of
the Lord Jesus to help Himself to our family. That is how the
Law is fulfilled in the Christian life. But how often it has been

neglected, and the people of God have failed in their duty. The Lord had a very strong word to say about this:

> Whoever then humbles himself as this child, he is the greatest in the kingdom of heaven. And whoever receives one such child in My name receives Me; but whoever causes one of these little ones who believe in Me to stumble, it is better for him that a heavy millstone be hung around his neck, and that he be drowned in the depth of the sea.
>
> Matthew 18:4–6

Notice those words "a heavy millstone." There are two kinds of millstones in the New Testament, the one on which the women would grind the corn, and another which was too big and heavy for that, so oxen were used to pull it. That is the word used here by the Lord. It is a dreadful thing to cause children to sin, and to hinder them from coming to the Saviour.

The answer to all this lies along one or two different lines. First of all, of course, by the honoring of the Lord in our own personal lives at home. That means that we do not always get baby-sitters while we go out to church. There is nothing honoring to the Lord in that. Have you ever heard your children say, "Dad, Mom, are you out to another meeting again?" Does that ever get at your heart? It does to mine. It is so easy to neglect the sacred, precious responsibility of the home.

How well do I remember when our older girl, as a small child, prayed one evening when we were praying together, "Lord Jesus, make me strong like my daddy." Then I tucked her in bed and came back later when she was asleep, and kneeling by her bedside I prayed, "Lord Jesus, please make me sweet and gentle like this little girl." How much we can learn from children's prayers if only we give time to listen to them! How much we miss when we miss just that!

That leads me to say that the most urgent necessity, perhaps, in some homes now is the repairing of the altar which has broken down, the restoring of family worship, when the whole family reads God's Word and prays together.

Once in my travels I was staying in a home, and early the first morning I heard a bell ring, followed by the scamper of feet. I thought I should follow the crowd, and found my way to the dining room, where I found a family of mother, father, and some ten children around a huge table. They were all there in various stages of dress and undress, some unshaven, some still in their night attire, but they were there. Father read to them a chapter from the Bible, made some comments on it; then he gave to each member of the family a missionary for whom he or she was to pray. We knelt by our chairs, and each person there prayed, from the parents to the youngest child. I found it all intensely moving, and found it hard to voice my thoughts as I prayed. The whole exercise took more than half an hour before breakfast, but it was like an anteroom to heaven. The father was a medical man, and shortly had to be in his office, but he had his priorities right, and his family came before his profession as he sought to bring them up in the nurture and knowledge of the Lord.

It is the responsibility of fathers to see to it that the family altar always comes first before anything, that the first priority is the prayer life of the family at home. What is the situation with your family altar? Is it broken down and neglected, or in daily use?

I saw statistics in the magazine *Christianity Today* showing that in the average evangelical church, of the total membership on the roll, 5% don't exist, 10% cannot be found, 25% never attend church, 50% have no missionary interest, 75% never attend church prayer meeting or Bible study, and 90% have no united family worship. If that is true, surely that is at the very root of the breakdown of society, of our homes and family life today.

That is something everyone can attend to immediately, repairing the altar that has broken down. What a wonderful thing it would be for children to see their parents once again meeting in prayer, worshiping the Lord, praising Him together, and the time of family worship restored.

Second, having repaired the family altar, demonstrate to family and children that love to Jesus comes first. This is the overall priority, that the love of Christ shines through the parents to them. In this way the wonderful circle commences—parents honoring the Lord should set the example to their children, who in turn will learn that their parents are to be trusted, and therefore are themselves to be honored. By the law of spiritual process (if there is such a thing!), as these children themselves come to trust and know the Lord for their direction in life, so as their parents grow old, they will recognize their responsibility toward them, and will find it their joy to look after them in their old age. Equally it is for the parents not to irritate or provoke their children at any stage in life, because that immediately alienates them, creates barriers and the oft-mentioned generation gap. Example is always better than precept, and therefore there is no better place for young people to come to know the Lord and to honor their parents than in the truly Christ-centered, Christ-loving, and Christ-serving home.

6

The Sixth Commandment:

LIFE IS SACRED

You shall not murder.   (Exodus 20:13)

In many translations this command comes as "You shall not kill," thus giving a complexity of thought on this subject, which in due course I will be seeking to elucidate, and on which I will be commenting.

These are four very simple and unmistakably clear words which have immense application and implication to the life of each one of us. We all know that we live in a world where life is cheap. There have been more people killed in road accidents than have been killed in two world wars. That fact does not seem to disturb us. We just take it for granted, and the fact that we are overshadowed by the imminent danger of a final catastrophic war is viewed purely from the angle of politics and expediency, without regard for these flaming words from heaven. I would that these four words could appear like fire in the sky so that all may recognize the sovereignty of God over human life.

However, that is not God's way of speaking. He has spoken in His Son, and Jesus is His last word to mankind (Hebrews 1:1–2). My prayer, therefore, is that the Holy Spirit might enable me to proclaim this Commandment in the light of its Old Testament setting, and also in its New Testament significance, in such a way that we may feel the force of it in our hearts and lives, and then through us to others.

First of all let us look at this law in its Old Testament obligation. This Commandment has to do with our relationship to our fellowmen, but this springs out of each person's relationship to God. God is the Father of all men only in the sense in which He is their Creator. He is, of course, the Father of the believer in a peculiar sense, when a person becomes a member of His redeemed family through faith in Jesus. Nevertheless, as Creator He is Father. The apostle Paul said while in Athens, "He [God] made from one, every nation of mankind to live on all the face of the earth . . . for in Him we live and move and exist, as even some of your own poets have said, 'For we also are His offspring' " (Acts 17:26–28). Therefore every human relationship is secondary to this one. The sanctity of marriage, the importance of character, the right of ownership—all stem from the fact of a Creator who has given to every man life and breath and all things. He is Sovereign Lord. The giving of life creates the possibility of every other relationship, and the cessation of life ends them all. Yes, every relationship owes its origin to the same source, and with the last breath of the body every other relationship is ended.

This Commandment, in a very simple way and yet in most definite language, flings a wall of fire around every human being and reserves to God, who first gave life, the right to end it. For the one relationship which death does not end is man's relationship to God. He has a purpose for every individual, each one of us, to be recognized here in time and realized in eternity. The issues of death are so great because of this fact that there could be no greater sin against humanity or against God than the taking of life. It is said, "life is cheap," but God says that life is sacred.

Paul again has a word to say about that:

> For not one of us lives for himself, and not one dies for himself; for if we live, we live for the Lord, or if we die, we die for the Lord; therefore whether we live or die, we are the Lord's. For to this end Christ died and lived again, that He might be Lord both of the dead and of the living. But you, why do you judge your brother? Or you again, why do you regard your brother with contempt? For we shall all stand before the judgment seat of God. For it is written, "As I LIVE, SAYS THE LORD, EVERY KNEE SHALL BOW TO ME, AND EVERY TONGUE SHALL GIVE PRAISE TO GOD." So then each one of us shall give account of himself to God.
>
> Romans 14:7–12

Life is sacred, and because it is, it is necessary to understand the difference between killing and murder, which is made very plain in the Old Testament. A clear distinction in the recognition of that helps greatly in understanding the Word of God in general, and this command in particular. Many people say they could never believe in a God who apparently was responsible for so much bloodshed, and therefore the God of the Old Testament is not the God of the New.

Numbers 35 plainly states the difference which God sets between killing and murder. All murder, of course, is killing, but all killing is not murder. In this chapter the Lord tells how, when His people finally possessed the land, six cities of refuge were to be provided in which a man who had unintentionally killed might find protection from the avenger of blood. If the killing was intentional, there was no protection whatsoever from revenge and punishment. Not that unintentional killing was to be taken lightly. Indeed the only safety for the one responsible for this action was for him to stay in a city of refuge during the lifetime of the high priest. To venture out would be to risk death at the hands of the avenger. But for the murderer who deliberately took the life of his fellowman there was no sanctuary at all: "The blood avenger himself shall put the murderer to death; he shall put him to death when he meets him" (Numbers 35:19).

Now if you are following carefully you may be saying that that is a contradiction to the Commandment which says "you shall not kill." If God reserves the right to end the life which He created, how could capital punishment be justified?

The answer, of course, lies in the understanding of the Old Testament economy. God had delegated to the Hebrew nation the right to maintain His law and His righteousness, and the death penalty was invoked at His express command upon certain sins. Whenever a man took the life of another, under the clearly defined conditions which God laid down, killing became the carrying out of the will of God through a human agency. An example of that is in Joshua 7, the story of Achan, who was stoned to death not by the will of man but by the will of God at the hands of men. The executioners were carrying out the express orders of heaven. No man, therefore, had ever a right to take life except when the Lord made him His agent to execute righteousness, and to rid the land of evil.

Now that fact explains the whole story of warfare in the Old Testament. The only justifiable war in history has been raised by divine command. And why should God command it? For the sole reason that He had a purpose for His land. That great purpose was a Bethlehem, a Calvary, an Ascension, a Pentecost; and everything that stood in the way of His redemptive plan must ultimately be destroyed. Over and over again He gave opportunity for repentance. When that remedy was refused, then He chose to make men the agents of His judgment; and when God's people went to war under those conditions, all the losses were on the side of the enemy. When they went to war on their own initiative they were slaughtered. Here, therefore, is the Sixth Commandment in relationship to its Old Testament obligation. In a word, no man had a right to take the life of another except by direct command from the Lord.

Now turn to the New Testament and its application of this law. The Lord Jesus, as I have said, came not to destroy the Law but to fulfill it. The only difference is that God, who once talked through the prophets, now speaks in His Son, and the whole ministry and teaching of Jesus magnifies this as well as any other command of God. No longer now does God speak through a nation. No longer, therefore, does He delegate His right to take a life to any human agency. He speaks to people individually concerning their personal relationship to Jesus Christ. No nation can say, "Our cause is a righteous one," for that term is purely comparative. The important thing, as Abraham Lincoln once said, is not is God on our side, but are we on His? Are we in agreement with Him concerning this law which He came to fulfill?

What did Jesus say about this Sixth Commandment? I remind you of certain verses in which He had something very definite to say.

In Luke 9:55 He rebuked His disciples for attempting to call down fire from heaven upon those who refused to hear Him.

In Matthew 26:52, when Peter made an eleventh-hour effort to stop what he thought was a tragedy, he took out his sword and cut off the ear of the high priest's servant (a very bad aim, because I am sure he meant to behead him!) the Lord said to him, "Put your sword back into its place; for all those who take up the sword shall perish by the sword."

In John 18:36, before Pontius Pilate, the Lord said, "My king-

dom is not of this world. If My kingdom were of this world,
then My servants would be fighting." In other words, Jesus
denounced war and killing—notice this—at the very point
where it was suggested for His own defense against the most
unholy alliance the world has ever known. It was through the
death of our Lord on an uplifted cross that men were to be
saved, and Jesus came not only to save the man who was sinned
against, but to save the sinner.

He came to redeem all men, and when one man kills another,
thrusting him into eternity, he inflicts the kind of punishment
upon him which shuts him off from all possibility of the redemptive grace of God.

I suggest to you that in the light of Christ's teaching, this law
becomes absolute. I find no justification for warfare, and
though it is a most controversial issue, that is why I find capital
punishment hard to accept. I fully recognize that until Jesus
comes again, war is inevitable in unregenerate society. He said
it would be: "And you will be hearing of wars and rumors of
wars . . ." (Matthew 24:6). One of the evidences of His imminent return will be a world at war constantly, because the outcome of the rejection of the Prince of Peace can only be strife
and warfare. I recognize that I am on very controversial territory
here, but this is the teaching of the Lord on this point as I see it.

At what point the duty of citizenship conflicts with the law of
God it is not for me to say. I believe that issue has to be settled
by every man in his own conscience before God. Some of my
greatest friends were outstanding leaders in World War II,
splendid soldiers and brave men who risked everything for the
sake of their country. I repeat, at what point the duties of citizenship conflict with the law of God is not for me to say. But I
thank God that the day shall come when the Lord shall set up
His reign of peace, and war shall be no more.

And He will judge between the nations . . .
And they will hammer their swords into plowshares,
    and their spears into pruning hooks.
Nation will not lift up sword against nation,
And never again will they learn war.

Isaiah 2:4

Oh, how eagerly we should watch and pray for that great day
when Jesus comes and puts a stop to it all! Many are asking,

"When do you think He will come?" Personally, I am not interested in a timetable but in a Person. I believe among evangelical Christians there ought to be a loving understanding that there are many different interpretations possible from the Word of God as to the precise time of His return.

Some great friends of mine believe that He may come at any time to take His people home. There will be a rapture when we will all be taken to heaven, then He will come to administer His reign on earth during the millennium. Other friends of mine believe there will be no millennium, but that He will come to set up His kingdom. Others again think He will come after the tribulation; some say He returns halfway through the tribulation, while others believe He will come when the millennium is all over. What a wide range of view there is among Christian people on this subject! But the great thing is that the Lord Jesus is coming to this earth personally, and before Him every knee shall bow and every tongue confess that He is Lord to the glory of God the Father (*see* Philippians 2:9–11).

Let me say one word more on the delicate subject of capital punishment. The Old Testament distinction between murder and killing is very relevant, and unquestionably the restoration of capital punishment would be a tremendous deterrent to crime. On the other hand, I cannot escape the fact already mentioned—that to end the life of anybody puts that person beyond all possible hope of the saving grace of God, and surely this is a matter which demands very careful thought and prayer.

Having discussed a somewhat controversial subject, let us concentrate upon the law "you shall not kill" and its present-day implications, because it leads to a personal application of all this to our hearts, and to a deeper aspect and meaning of the command which we have not yet considered.

The implications of it affect both the world and the Church—both the believer and the unbeliever—because unsaved and saved are all guilty and condemned by this command. Right at the heart of the revelation of the Bible is a record of a murder for which the whole world is guilty. Jesus had come into a dark, hopeless sort of world to bring deliverance. He made it clear that while forgiveness and salvation were the free gift of God's grace on the ground of His atoning blood which He shed at Calvary, no man could ever come to Him unless he was prepared to accept His standards of living, His ethics, His own standard of morality. He has bid all His followers take His yoke upon them and learn of Him.

His great purpose is to demonstrate His life to the world until He comes again. He is going to reveal His kingdom on earth through a company of blood-bought people, redeemed humanity indwelt by God, who would show the world the thrill of living in the Kingdom. Now do not put off the Kingdom until the millennial age. If you have the King in your heart, you are a citizen of the Kingdom. God is seeking to infiltrate society today with men and women, a blood-bought humanity, obedient citizens of His kingdom, to demonstrate the freedom of life lived under the bondage of the Lord Jesus.

The Lord has not come to offer us an easy way out of our problems. He is not going to sneak us into the back door of heaven as if He were ashamed of us! No, indeed: His blood-bought children will receive a royal welcome at the Pearly Gates of Glory, because He is proud of those who have been saved by grace, indwelt by His Spirit, and made pure by His life. He, by His perfect life, set before the world of His day the highest kind of ethics, the complete fulfillment of His law in human experience, but the men of His day could not face it: the price was too great. The example and challenge of His purity had to be obliterated, so His voice was silenced, the challenge of His life was rejected, and they hounded Him to death.

May I say that that is exactly what happens to a Spirit-filled Christian today? If anyone in your circle of friends is neutral about Jesus, there is perhaps something wrong with your witness. The very challenge of your life will mean that people take sides. Some will be for you, some against you; but you will share in the rejection of Christ. You cannot be popular in heaven and popular in the world, for that is absolutely impossible. They put Him to death. That may not happen to you literally, but they will do something very much like it. If you are finding yourself in a hot seat, having a rough time either in your work or in your home because you are redeemed and standing up for Jesus, then thank Him. I am not sorry for you! I am not being unkind, but I praise God that your witness is so clear-cut that nobody can be neutral. This does not mean you are offensive to people, but that you are consistent in your stand for Jesus, and your way of life demands an answer from those among whom you live and work.

Let not the death of Jesus be laid on the shoulders of a former generation:

> This Man, delivered up by the predetermined plan and foreknowledge of God, you nailed to a cross by the hands of godless men and put Him to death. And God raised Him up again . . . . This Jesus God raised up again, to which we are all witnesses . . . . Therefore let all the house of Israel know for certain that God has made Him both Lord and Christ—this Jesus whom you crucified.
>
> Acts 2:23, 24, 32, 36

That absolutely shattered the people in conviction, as they heard Peter preach on the day of Pentecost. Yet we are as guilty, for every time you and I turn our backs upon Jesus we repeat it all over again. Every violation of conscience, every time I willfully sin, I drive another nail into His hands, for He died to save me from that. Every time I reject Him, I crucify Him afresh. For that cruel, murderous death we too are guilty. Judgment has yet to be executed. The only thing that delays it is the marvel of God's love and grace. The mystery and wonder of the gospel is that into that awful act of violent death wrought upon the Son of God, God the Father has woven the wonderful plan of His salvation. I am saved by hiding in the very wounds that I am responsible for inflicting! Wonderful grace of Jesus! The blood of Jesus, drawn by sinners, is a fountain for their cleansing. All the same, the sentence of judgment will yet be pronounced and executed: "The Lord is not slow about His promise, as some count slowness, but is patient toward you, not wishing for any to perish but for all to come to repentance" (2 Peter 3:9).

But the most heart-searching application of this Commandment is to be in the life of the believer:

> You have heard that the ancients were told, "You shall not commit murder," and "Whoever commits murder shall be liable to the court." But I say to you that every one who is angry with his brother shall be guilty before the court; and whoever shall say to his brother, "Raca," shall be guilty before the supreme court; and whoever shall say, "You fool," shall be guilty enough to go into the hell of fire. If therefore you are presenting your offer-

ing at the altar, and there remember that your brother
has something against you, leave your offering there before the altar, and go your way; first be reconciled to your
brother, and then come and present your offering.

Matthew 5:21–24

What do you think those words say to Christians today? You
see, that is Christ's law for members of His family in the Kingdom. The Sermon on the Mount is His law for His people, and
here from it murder is traced to its ugly source. The Saviour is
interested not only in knocking the gun out of a man's hand,
but in taking the devil out of his heart. "You have heard it said
. . . but I say to you . . . .": until a believer has learned the
meaning of that, he has never begun to worship. The whole
force of the Holy Spirit's convicting is directed against sin and
hatred—or rather against the man and his guilt—and he finds
himself under the sovereignty of Jesus. When a man is there, it
is impossible for murder to lurk in his heart, for it is counted as
sin even to think evil of another.

"Lord, what shall I do?" we may well cry.

"Every one who is angry with his brother shall be guilty . . . .
If you are presenting your offering at the altar, and there remember that your brother has something against you, leave
your offering there . . . first be reconciled to your brother." Do
you notice the threefold use of the word *brother?*

See how this Old Testament Commandment spoken so long
ago comes right down to us here and now, and strikes right in
the heart, because forgiveness makes great demands upon us.
The cross of Jesus where I find forgiveness does not only offer
me atonement, it demands the example of Jesus. Upon the
foundation of the atonement, by the power of His Spirit, the
character of Christ has to be built. The Bible demands a high
performance from people who have been forgiven. The evidence of having been forgiven by Jesus will be very clear, because the forgiven person will always forgive others. In
Matthew 6:14, 15—following the family prayer (the Lord's
prayer is surely in John 17) in which the Lord teaches us to pray
"forgive us . . . as we forgive,"—is the only comment the Lord
makes upon any section of the model prayer: "For if you forgive
men their transgressions, your heavenly Father will also forgive

you. But if you do not forgive men, then your Father will not forgive your transgressions."

Do you hold a grudge against anyone whom you refuse to forgive? With all the authority of the Word behind me, I say you are proclaiming to all that God has never forgiven you. You cannot refuse to forgive somebody else if you claim to be a child of God. You cannot say, "I'll never speak to that person again!"

Simon Peter once asked the Lord, "Lord, how often shall my brother sin against me and I forgive him? Up to seven times?" (Matthew 18:21).

I am sure Peter thought that was being almost overgenerous, but Jesus said to him, "I do not say to you up to seven times, but up to seventy times seven" (verse 22). That means no limit—490 times; so try that, Simon! There is no limit to the saving grace of the Lord Jesus to us when we fail, therefore we must never limit our forgiveness of other people.

Apply that in your church life and you would have revival. Many churches are split from top to bottom because of people who refuse to forgive one another. So often they carry these differences to the absurd, unbiblical extreme of hiving off and forming another little independent Bible-believing church marked "separate." The history of the average church of that kind can usually be traced to a split through Christians who have refused to forgive each other, who are empty of love.

My friend, when you receive God's mercy in forgiveness it is not given in a cup, but you receive it through a pipeline from an inexhaustible supply. It is not given to be held for oneself, but we receive it in overflowing abundance to pass on to others. The greatest thing we can ever be in our lives is a stepping-stone to Jesus, and stepping-stones are designed to be walked on, and that hurts, especially if those who walk on us are our friends. That is why it takes a crucified man to witness to a crucified Christ. The man who has an unforgiving spirit is simply telling far and wide that he has never been forgiven himself.

"You shall not kill": if you hold a grudge, and if your brother has something against you (that means that you are right and he is wrong), then, says the Master, when you come and worship, leave your gifts, which I cannot accept until you go and be reconciled to your brother. So many of our prayers get no

higher than the roof and never reach the heavens, simply because those praying together for God's blessing and reviving
power are those who never speak to one another at all. Again
may I say, a man who is forgiven does not go on sinning. God
does not make it impossible for us to sin, but He always makes
it possible for us not to sin.

Oswald Chambers, in his great book *My Utmost for His Highest*, says, "Either sin or God must die out in my life. The New
Testament brings me to this one issue: if sin rules in me, then
God's life in me will be killed. If God rules in me, then sin will
be killed. This is the great ultimate. Sin crucified Christ and still
does. 'For if you are living according to the flesh, you must die;
but if by the Spirit you are putting to death the deeds of the
body, you shall live' (Romans 8:13)."

This is exciting! I know that every day I live until I get to
heaven I have a moral responsibility before God that when
there comes to my mind and heart some thought of hatred,
some bitterness, some resentment, I look up to the Lord and
say, "Lord Jesus, this belongs to the old self-life, but You died
and rose again to deliver me from that in order to introduce me
to the life of Your kingdom. This thought of hatred is of Satan,
not of You, but Lord, I cannot do a thing about it; that is what I
am, and I always will be the same. I cannot help being resentful
with people, but Lord, I thank You that I want this thing to die,
so I hand it over to You for execution." The Holy Spirit then
carries out the sentence of death, and lives in my heart to reveal
the love and forgiveness of Jesus to others.

Now bring to your mind those people to whom you have not
spoken, and against whom you hold resentment. They are
perhaps in your church, and you know that the fellowship is
being wrecked by your cold, hard, harsh attitude in the breaking of this Commandment. Lift your heart to God and say,
"Lord Jesus, as I think about these people, Satan is trying to
show me the kind of person I really am. But thank You, Lord,
that You told me about that a long time ago. You know all about
me, and You thought me worth dying for. Therefore, Lord, I
want all this to die out, and I hand it over to the Holy Spirit. I
am trusting Him to carry out in my life the sentence of death
and to flood my heart with Your love shed abroad by the Holy
Spirit."

It is positively amazing what will happen when you put your

arm around that person to whom you have not spoken for weeks and say "I love you!" You will not be able to believe yourself, and maybe he won't either! But you will prove its reality and demonstrate it by your actions and by your life. That is a miracle. That is what this poor old world needs to see, the love of Christ in members of His family. The person who is forgiven not only forgives others, not only does he learn not to do this thing again, not to go on sinning, but he is under tremendous obligation to tell others. He is debtor to all men to spread the message of the love of God in Jesus, to tell them of One who not only takes the gun out of his hand but, praise God, takes the devil out of his heart!

What a message for the twentieth century to hear from your lips! May people hear it from a life that is transformed by His love.

7

The Seventh Commandment:

THE PERMANENCE OF MARRIAGE

You shall not commit adultery.   (Exodus 20:14)

As the previous Commandment had to do with the sacredness of human life, so this one puts a flaming sword around the only relationship on earth which has power to bring life into existence. God's first circle of society is the family: "And God created man in His own image . . . male and female He created them" (Genesis 1:27).

The origin of the family in the purpose of God lies within the union of the man and the woman. Man, woman, child: that is God's eternal triangle, the base on which the pyramid of life is raised. Every other relationship in life—racial, political, social—springs out of this one. How essential it is, therefore, for the well-being of all society that this, the source of every other relationship, should be carefully guarded against all abuse. The Law in the Old Testament had no forgiveness for adultery: the guilty party must be put to death (Leviticus 20:10).

The unity and union of the man and the woman are the real expression of God's image. He made man in His own image, not the man or the woman alone, but male and female He made them, after His own likeness.

This helps us to understand, I think, the great thrust of this command, which forbids all unchastity. If the union of the man and the woman is always in the plan of God, then it is not merely the fulfillment of a marriage ceremony which puts an end to all unfaithfulness. Premarital sex is a sin against the marriage that is about to be. There is no Commandment more difficult to deal with faithfully, but I am sure there is none which needs so much honest and fearless handling in the light of the permissiveness of today.

Let me ask you to think of this command itself as it stands: "You shall not . . . ." There is no reason given and no argument used, of course, because none is required, for this sin is so destructive within itself—which is sufficient cause for the stern "you shall not." It is a sin, in the first place, against the individual. Nature visits this sin with heavy penalty. You and I know perfectly well the awful results in the purely physical realm, the grim effect that this has upon the people involved, often causing complete mental, physical, and emotional breakdown.

Spiritual usefulness has been ruined many times by the unlawful yielding to this sin. More than once—indeed I tremble to think just how many times—I have sat at my desk, and across from me has been a pastor, a Christian leader, a teacher of God's Word, absolutely broken because he has fallen to this sin and has come out of the ministry. The balance of soul and spirit and body is absolutely destroyed by this sin, and the man who falls into immoral habits commits, inevitably, spiritual suicide. It is firstly a sin against the individual.

It is also a sin against the family. The sacredness of motherhood and childhood is secured by marriage, and when this Commandment is broken and the sanctity of that relationship is violated, God's provision for both mother and child is broken. When the family is broken as a whole, who can tell the harm that is done to the children? One reads stories every day in the newspaper which tell of granting a decree with custody of the children given to one parent, and there you read the destruction of the family after God's pattern. In many a modern daily paper, indeed, are the birth, marriage, and death announcements, and alongside them the column of "Marriages Dissolved." The ultimate tragedy is that this situation is so accepted by society now that not an eyebrow is raised, and scarcely a tear is shed at the heartbreak there must be behind those cold words, not only of the man and woman involved, but also for the children who are so often members of a one-parent family, launched to restart life among peers who rejoice in having two parents.

It is a sin against society, because society is just a union of families. Every attempt to create society on any other basis than that is disastrous. The sin which blights marriage and destroys the family is the enemy of all society.

Furthermore, it is a sin against the nation. The greatness of a country depends on the purity, strength, and character of its people. In any nation where the marriage relationship is violated, destructive forces strike the very heart and core of that nation's life. The adulterer is the greatest enemy of the state. The Communist world recognizes this, because how often we read of diplomats in the Eastern bloc who are put into compromising situations, photographed in them, and then receive the visible proof of their folly, which is used as either personal or political blackmail. The evil forces of communism fully recognize the power of sex, and employ its implications to wreck lives, and ultimately the nations to which the unfortunate men belong.

No Christian minister has the right to remarry the man or woman at whose door lies the guilt of severing a marriage relationship. Even if he is imprisoned for the rest of his life, the one guilty of adultery could not wipe out the wrong done in striking a blow at the sanctity of the family. "Righteousness exalts a nation, but sin is a disgrace to any people" (Proverbs 14:34).

Not only is adultery a sin against the nation, it is a sin against the whole race. The union of mankind is not a dream but a fact. Heredity is a tremendous reality. "For as through the one man's disobedience the many were made sinners . . ." (Romans 5:19)—that is the root of all evil. "Even so through the obedience of the One the many will be made righteous" (Romans 5:19b)—that is the root of our redemption.

The heredity of sin is natural and negative. The heredity of righteousness is supernatural and positive. In our redemption God replaces the downward drag of degeneration by the upward pull of regeneration. Every life contributes its share to the forces which either make or mar mankind. Every man or woman guilty of this sin inflicts deadly wounds on a generation that is yet unborn. Alas, in the interest of a present moment, in the surge of unholy passion and desire, the cry of unborn babes is unheard. "You shall not commit adultery."

Most of all, this is a sin against God. If every man is made in His image, if in every family God is the true Head, of all human society He is the Shepherd, over every nation He is King, and the whole race is His to the uttermost limit, it is therefore by necessity of His awesome holiness that the abominable, the whoremongers, have their part eternally in the lake that burns with fire, which is the second death (Revelation 21:8).

"Let marriage be held in honor among all, and let the marriage bed be undefiled; for fornicators and adulterers God will judge" (Hebrews 13:4).

"Do not be deceived; neither fornicators, nor idolaters, nor adulterers, nor effeminate, nor homosexuals . . . shall inherit the kingdom of God" (1 Corinthians 6:9, 10).

Now consider the Commandment as it stands today. I hardly need to say how important the emphasis on this law is, because how blatant is the tendency to loosen the binding nature of marriage. It is regarded these days simply as a civil relationship entered into by state laws, and revoked by the same easy procedure. But that is just not true. The lawfulness of marriage lies within the fact of sex, and sex is God's creation. He alone has the right to condition the the law of union between man and woman. All too frequently marriage is entered into without any recognition of God. No wonder there is misery and tears. No wonder no one can tamper with the things of God without being harmed. Once this sacred union of marriage is consummated, it is a union for life. There is only one reason for annulling marriage before death, and that is a more awful thing than death itself—adultery. The idea that incompatibility is sufficient to dissolve marriage is a blow at the throne of God.

In the Western world, pornographic literature in which marriage relationships are prostituted, television programs making mockery of Christian marriage, and a general attitude of cynicism toward marriage for life, are all flung at our society. Interestingly enough, such things are banned in communist countries. They export literature to the West because Russia and China know perfectly well that they will never need to declare war against the United States or Britain. They have said long ago that those countries will collapse from within. One of the tenets of Stalin was to so demoralize a nation from within that, should it ever become necessary to fight, victory will be easy. And how well this strategy has succeeded in so many parts of the world, including our Western democratic system. Pornographic literature stocked in far too many bookstores in every city and town of our land, read not only by teenagers but by older people too, drags down the morals and the will-power of a country to resist enemies.

Apart from pornographic literature, marriage relationships today are prostituted because of the flinging together of both sexes in forms of employment which lead to sinful relationships, or can do so. And if I may be pardoned for saying so, the fashion of dress which is suggestive rather than attractive, and which is all out of harmony with the reverence a man should have for a woman, all adds fuel to the fire of passion. I would lovingly say to every Christian girl: Take care; think it out alone with God, and decide what and how to dress in attire which is neither prudish nor suggestive, which reveals primarily the imparted beauty of Jesus rather than the applied beauty of the drugstore, so that a man is attracted by what he sees of the living Lord Jesus in you.

What has the New Testament to say about this command?

> And some Pharisees came to Him [the Lord Jesus], testing Him, and saying, "Is it lawful for a man to divorce his wife for any cause at all?"
>
> And He answered and said, "Have you not read, that He who created them from the beginning MADE THEM MALE AND FEMALE, and said, 'FOR THIS CAUSE A MAN SHALL LEAVE HIS FATHER AND MOTHER, AND SHALL CLEAVE TO HIS WIFE; AND THE TWO SHALL BECOME ONE FLESH'?
>
> "Consequently they are no more two, but one flesh. What therefore God has joined together, let no man separate."
>
> They said to Him, "Why then did Moses command to GIVE HER A CERTIFICATE AND DIVORCE HER?"
>
> He said to them, "Because of your hardness of heart, Moses permitted you to divorce your wives; but from the beginning it has not been this way. And I say to you, whoever divorces his wife, except for immorality, and marries another commits adultery."
>
> Matthew 19:3–9

Jesus was answering the question of the Pharisees concerning divorce. That is a subject which would require many hours of teaching and much fair treatment, but it is not the subject of this study. However, it must be mentioned in this context without amplification. In the New Testament it is perfectly plain that divorce is allowed only on the grounds of adultery, as the passage quoted shows. The marriage tie cannot be broken scripturally on any other basis than that. The remarriage of a guilty party is forbidden, and the one who marries such becomes guilty also.

> And it was said, "WHOEVER DIVORCES HIS WIFE, LET HIM GIVE HER A CERTIFICATE OF DISMISSAL"; but I say to you that every one who divorces his wife, except for the cause of unchastity, makes her commit adultery; and whoever marries a divorced woman commits adultery.
>
> Matthew 5:31, 32

To divorce your partner, says the Lord Jesus, on any other grounds, and to remarry, is adultery. The remarriage of an innocent partner is permitted, provided the previous partner is dead or has married again, and in marrying again has committed adultery.

> For the married woman is bound by law to her husband while he is living; but if her husband dies, she is released from the law concerning the husband. So then if, while her husband is living, she is joined to another man, she shall be called an adulteress; but if her husband dies, she is free from the law, so that she is not an adulteress, though she is joined to another man.
>
> Romans 7:2, 3

This subject must be left there, though no doubt many questions arise which cannot be dealt with fully here. I can only bear testimony to this fact as a minister of the Word of God. When I have confronted people in this situation my heart has gone out to them in love. No minister can ever know the full facts and what has led to the tragedy and breakdown in two lives. I always err on the side of mercy where it is possible. I have actually remarried the innocent party of a divorce more than once, after careful counseling and seeking to understand and really to know who is the innocent party, because this is very difficult to ascertain.

But Jesus in this passage of Scripture goes far beyond the law of Moses to the law of God, at the very beginning of creation,

when the Lord created woman to be a helpmeet to man, saying,
"For this cause a man shall leave his father and his mother, and
shall cleave to his wife; and they shall become one flesh"
(Genesis 2:24). And the Lord Jesus added, "What therefore God
has joined together, let no man separate" (Matthew 19:6).

Marriage is not a civil contract; it is a sacrament. It is something in which a man and a woman become one flesh. Something new has taken place. Ties at home are broken; father and
mother are left in order that a man and woman may be joined
together as one, and what God has put together no man is to
separate. There is a permanent union about that which runs
right through Scripture. Paul says that the awful thing about
fornication is that a man becomes one flesh with a harlot (see 1
Corinthians 6:16). What a solemn word! No human or man-
made law can break a blood relationship. Even though a boy is
disowned, he is always a son. Marriage is a blood relationship
which cannot be made void. It is provided for in the creation of
the human body, and no law on earth can break it. It is not
merely the establishment of a partnership but the institution of
a relationship from which there is no turning back.

Let me define the ideal home: one plus one equals one (not
two) plus Jesus. In the matter of adultery the Lord goes far
behind the act to the thought, for the most penetrating word in
the New Testament has yet to be said. Remember too it comes
not from the lips of a preacher, but from the Lord Jesus Himself:

> You have heard that it was said, "YOU SHALL NOT
> COMMIT ADULTERY"; but I say to you, that every one who
> looks on a woman to lust for her has committed adultery
> with her already in his heart. And if your right eye
> makes you stumble, tear it out, and throw it from you;
> for it is better for you that one of the parts of your body
> perish, than for your whole body to be thrown into hell.
> Matthew 5:27–29

That is very straight talking. The Pharisees had reduced the
Commandment to the actual act of adultery, and imagined that
as long as they were not guilty of that act it had nothing whatever to say to them. That is because they had never read the Ten
Commandments properly. If they had, they would have discovered that you cannot take one Commandment in isolation apart

from the rest. For instance, the Tenth Commandment says, "You shall not covet your neighbor's wife." The law of God does not stop at actions but challenges desires. Sin fools us to imagine we may be satisfied as long as we are not guilty of the act. Many who never commit the act of adultery enjoy sinning in their mind. Is it only because of social interest that we read details of every divorce suit in the press? What about the paperbacks that are full of sex and perversions? Do people read them out of mere philosophical interest, or because by proxy in reading them they are sinning in imagination? Why do even Christian people sit up at night to watch the late night show on television, which is so often verging on the pornographic, and thus ruin their devotional times? You cannot meet God in prayer early in the morning if you watch that sort of filth at night. A Christian has to know what it is to discipline his life that he might grow in stature and in likeness to the Lord Jesus.

That is why I believe sex morality ought to be taught by parents and not by schoolteachers. The tragedy of modern education is that it is based on philosophy which does not admit sin. To teach a child what he does not know about the facts of life without explaining to him the sinfulness of his heart is imparting knowledge to him which can easily lead to sin in his life. I am sure that no one can excuse a parent for failure in fulfilling the responsibility of proclaiming the fact of sin and the need of God's salvation to his precious children.

Our Lord goes behind the act to the thought, behind the deed to the desire, and condemns it. Do you notice in that passage He says it is better to maim the body, to cut off hand or eye? The body is precious, but not so precious as purity of heart and spirit. At all cost, this law of God has to be obeyed, and here is the great battleground of life. Jesus knew full well that it is unchastity of thought that ruins spiritual growth, and therefore He emphasizes this law with renewed force. Grace is no cheap, easy way out. Grace heightens and enforces and reinforces the law of God. "You have heard it said, 'You shall not commit adultery,' but I say unto you . . ." and He goes right to the root of it all.

He is not interested in stopping the line at the divorce court. He is concerned with creating happy Christian homes, therefore He said there must be no trifling with this. How is it to be done? I am sure there is not a person anywhere who would like to have the history of his life put on a screen for all the world to see. Is there therefore no word of hope, or word of assurance in forgiveness? Oh, yes, there is! I am so thankful this study does not have to end on a severe note, for there would be no hope for anybody. That is why I would share with you the wonderful story in John 8:3–11:

> And the scribes and the Pharisees brought a woman caught in adultery, and having set her in the midst, they said to Him, "Teacher, this woman has been caught in adultery, in the very act. Now in the Law Moses commanded us to stone such women; what then do You say?"
> And they were saying this, testing Him, in order that they might have grounds for accusing Him. But Jesus stooped down, and with His finger wrote on the ground. But when they persisted in asking Him, He straightened up, and said to them, "He who is without sin among you, let him be the first to throw a stone at her."
> And again He stooped down, and wrote on the ground. And when they heard it, they began to go out one by one, beginning with the older ones, and He was left alone, and the woman, where she had been, in the midst.
> And straightening up, Jesus said to her, "Woman, where are they? Did no one condemn you?"
> And she said, "No one, Lord." And Jesus said, "Neither do I condemn you; go your way; from now on sin no more."

Jesus was preaching in the temple early in the morning, and they brought a woman taken in the very act of adultery. Oh, those Pharisees! I don't want to take off on a tangent, but we have their equivalent today. How unkind Christian people are to one another! We have forgiveness for the sinner but precious little for the child of God who falls. How merciful we can be to those who do not know the Lord, but how censorious we are to the Christian who has been tripped up.

Here the Pharisees brought this woman taken in the act, thinking they had really caught the Lord in a trap. "Moses said . . . . What do You say?" And Jesus stooped to write on the ground. This is the only record in the Bible of the Lord writing, and through the centuries people have wondered what He wrote. The Pharisees persisted in their question, but Jesus just raised Himself (can you picture it?) and looking them full in the face said, "He who is without sin among you, let him be the first to throw a stone at her." And they went out, from the oldest to the youngest. The oldest went first, probably because they were the most guilty, and the younger ones followed. Can you picture them all trooping out without a word? Their whole argument had crashed to the ground, and Jesus was left alone with the woman. He said to her, "Woman [and on the lips of Jesus that is a word of tremendous love], where are they? Did no one condemn you?" "No man, Lord." No one calls Jesus Lord but by the Holy Spirit. The contrast between the Pharisees, with all their hardness and coldness, and the wonderful way in which Jesus had disposed of them, had brought into that woman's life a radiance, a hope, an assurance that He is Lord of every situation.

Then there came words from His lips that must have been like rivers of living water: "Neither do I condemn you; go your way; from now on sin no more."

Now Jesus did not excuse or condone sin, nor did He condemn the sinner, but He separates the act, which He condemns, from the sinner, whom He forgives. The Law has no forgiveness for adultery, but the Lord Jesus has: "But there is forgiveness with Thee, That Thou mayest be feared" (Psalms 130:4).

He is ready to forgive, and He is ready to empower. But of course He needs to be shown that there is genuine repentance, and that the sinner means business.

"You shall not commit adultery"—that is the command.

"Do not let sin reign in your mortal body"—that is the promise in Romans 6:12.

"You shall receive power when the Holy Spirit has come upon you"—that is the power to overcome given by the Lord (Acts 1:8).

Finally I would say to someone who is absolutely without hope, with a broken heart and a broken home, who may be at the end of his rope about this very thing, for he knows he is guilty: Remember that Jesus has forgiveness, but if you would know the experience of His delivering power you must learn to reject every claim of sin, because there is a fire in your heart if you stay near enough to it. Don't read the book that stimulates you to sin—burn it. Get rid of all that fosters the fire of passion, clear out your bookshelves and your records of all that drags you down. Exercise knob control of your TV, look at nothing that would dim your vision of the Lord Jesus, and obey Philippians 4:8.

Then reckon on the mighty Conqueror of sin, the Lord Jesus, who gives forgiveness full and free, who comes to your defeated heart to indwell it with His life. Remember, "it is God who is at work in you, both to will and to work for His good pleasure" (Philippians 2:13). That is His side. "Work out your salvation with fear and trembling" (Philippians 2:12). That is your side. When He sees your willingness and desire to work out what He has worked in by His Holy Spirit, then there is power in His name, deliverance, and total victory.

8

The Eighth Commandment:
RIGHT OF OWNERSHIP

You shall not steal. (Exodus 20:15)

You will notice the course which these Ten Commandments follow. The first four are specifically concerned with our relationship to God. The next three safeguard the most sacred relationship of human life, the family circle. At the same time they reserve the right of God, who created life, to end it. The last three Commandments have to do primarily with property; and penalties for breaking these are less severe, not because they are not important but simply because a man's life consists not in the abundance of things he possesses (Luke 12:15).

It is a striking commentary on human nature that human laws have reversed all this. Breakdown in relationship with God does not seem to matter. Godlessness is popular these days; perhaps it is at the root of every other crime which the law courts punish heavily. The crime for which the law inflicts punishment is not nearly as harmful as that which it cannot touch—our relationship with God.

This fact is clearly illustrated in the Eighth Commandment. There are many different ways of stealing, but the root of them all is this:

> Do you not know that your body is a temple of the Holy Spirit who is in you, whom you have from God, and that you are not your own? For you have been bought with a price: therefore glorify God in your body.
>
> 1 Corinthians 6:19, 20

While the actual act of stealing is recognized, of course, as wrong, to deny God His rightful ownership of our lives, which He has purchased at Calvary, is excused on a thousand different levels of argument. Yet every instance of theft can be traced to this source and can be found to be due to failure to submit to the control of the Holy Spirit in our personal lives.

As we think now about this Eighth Commandment we shall see that it has a lot more to say about things other than with the pilfering of another's property, of which few of us are guilty. It has much to do with robbing God of His rightful ownership of life and not allowing Him to possess His inheritance in His people, and at the same time our robbing Him of our availability by failing to press home for our inheritance in Him. You rob God in these ways.

The command itself states "you shall not steal," so obviously man is given the right of possession, or theft would be impossible. There are only four ways in which you can possess anything: by inheritance, by gift, by work, and by stealing. Now this Commandment recognizes the first three but forbids the fourth, because the first three are based on laws which are essential to love and service, and indeed to all relationships.

The gift by inheritance is an expression of love, and becomes the property of the person who receives it. Service and work earn their legitimate reward, and that reward is the property of the one who earns it. But theft violates all that. The thief does not work for the person from whom he steals, nor does he earn what he acquires. This Commandment therefore recognizes the right of ownership by love and work, but forbids ownership on any other basis—so, "you shall not steal."

Once again, in this command as in all the others, it is reinforced with tremendous significance in the New Testament. Grace is found to be no diluting of law but rather the imparting of a new life in Christ. Jesus' obedience to the Law is reckoned ours, and His obedient life is given to us that we also may obey the Law. Such is the wonderful grace of Jesus!

Hear the New Testament enforcing this Commandment: "Let him who steals steal no longer; but rather let him labor, performing with his own hands what is good, in order that he may have something to share with him who has need" (Ephesians 4:28).

You see, on the one hand stealing is forbidden; while on the other, labor and love, working and giving, are presented as the only true way of ownership.

But the New Testament carries it still further, for in this verse Paul states very clearly that whatever is gained by work is not for our own selfish enjoyment. Rather it is for helping others who are less fortunate than ourselves: that you may have something to share with him who has need. The logic of that is clear. There are many people who have not the ability or the power to work, and if this principle of the Law is not followed, they will be forced to steal to get what they need. Furthermore, the person who works for his own satisfaction only is stealing if he fails to distribute to those in need.

Nobody puts the crown on Jesus' head if he lives for himself and ignores the needs of others. Therefore, how must this command be applied today? First of all, it exposes the wrong of a condition which forbids a man to own his own property, however small or large. There is a right of private ownership in the law of God. The socialist state denies that.

Again, it denies the right of ownership except by gift or service, and this law finds guilty all who possess anything which they have obtained other than by a free gift from someone, or in return for work. Of course, the open act of stealing is frowned upon. Yet there are many who have never committed that act who are still guilty, for the commandment which governs so much of commercial life today is not "you shall not steal" but "you shall not be found out." That is the "eleventh commandment," really!

In a permissive society you can get away with anything; people believe in situational ethics these days, but if you are such a fool as to be found out, then it is too bad. Trickery, dishonesty, lying are looked upon as smartness. The whole habit of gambling is the very essence of theft for the reason that by gambling a person comes to possess something which is a total violation of labor and love. A gambler receives money for which he does not work, and by doing so he robs the one through whom he receives it.

Drink and gambling have taken over in so many countries and, alas, are the goal and occupation of far too many people, young and old. The lust for possession without work lies at the root of it all, and is at the back of so much that saps strength and morality from the lives of men and women, and therefore of a whole nation. More pay and less work. Never has a generation grabbed at so much for so little, and that is the outcome of failure to observe this Eighth Commandment.

The truth must be brought nearer home, however, for stealing is not only something which affects people, it affects God: "Will a man rob God?" (Malachi 3:8). Here is the most serious position of all.

How does a man rob God? Well, in several ways, though only a few can be mentioned here. First of all in careless stewardship, particularly in reference to money. None of us has a right to all that he earns. God's portion under the Law was one-tenth. Surely grace demands more. The disciplined giving of every Christian brings immense blessing. "Your heavenly Father knows that you need all these things. But seek first His kingdom and His righteousness; and all these things shall be added to you" (Matthew 6:32, 33).

God's blessing in and through the lives of His people is so often thwarted and His promises go unclaimed because they break this Commandment by careless stewardship, and so often by giving to the Lord's work less than a waitress in a restaurant would be tipped. Remember, the Lord says "you shall not steal."

This Commandment is also broken in failure to make a total consecration and commitment of our lives to Him. I owe my life, and you owe yours, to the Lord Jesus. He wants your brain to think through, your hands to work through, your feet to run and walk for Him, your heart to radiate His love. He wants the talents and gifts you possess, for they are His. They belong to Him, because He created you and them. To hold those talents to yourself He regards as stealing. Who is using them? Who is controlling your brain, hands, feet, heart, gifts? Have you ever brought them to the Lord and handed them over to Him completely, or do you insist on using them for yourself and claiming ownership of them?

The cross is God's great plea, as was seen in 1 Corinthians 6:19, 20, which is a statement to grip one's heart as you realize you are *bought*. The Lord does not say that He has "kept" or "made" you, but that He has "bought" you. The greatest plea for your surrender is that God has bought you not with perishable things like silver or gold, but through the precious blood of

Christ (1 Peter 1:18, 19). What a price Jesus paid as He bared His back to the lash which was due to us, and to the nails of the cross, as He bore the pain of our judgment. The greatest fact in all history is that I have been bought—I am not my own. And because of Calvary, God has an inheritance in my life that He wants to use.

> For this reason I too, having heard of the faith in the Lord Jesus which exists among you, and your love for all the saints, do not cease giving thanks for you, while making mention of you in my prayers; that the God of our Lord Jesus Christ, the Father of glory, may give to you a spirit of wisdom and of revelation in the knowledge of Him.
> I pray that the eyes of your heart may be enlightened, so that you may know what is the hope of His calling, what are the riches of the glory of His inheritance in the saints, and what is the surpassing greatness of His power toward us who believe.
>
> Ephesians 1:15–19

God has an inheritance in us that He wants to claim and to use. If that is true, then I have no right to myself. I have no right to injure myself, to uncleanness, to self-indulgence. I have no right to let my gifts lie wasted, or to use them without reference to the One who gave them to me. I have to ask Him whether that natural gift is one which He can use, then I have to take it to the cross that there it might be cleansed and anointed with His Spirit. You might have the gift of speech or oratory, but that does not make you a preacher necessarily. You might have the gift of singing, but that does not of necessity make you a gospel soloist. You may have a gift for playing a trumpet, or the piano, or any other instrument, but that does not make you a Christian musician. If you are prepared to take every gift you may have naturally and lay it at the foot of the cross, God will give back to you in resurrection life those gifts which He wants to use.

There is a great difference between a sermon and a message. A sermon can have introduction, three points, and conclusion, all beginning with the same letter, all perfectly correct, but it can be dead—just a performance. There is nothing more killing than that, orthodoxy without life. Similarly, a solo which is not touched by the Holy Spirit has no ministry in power; but when the soloist has really taken that gift of voice to the Lord and He has given it back, then the outflow in song is touched with a new dimension.

Preaching is really the communication of truth through a personality, and it may be communicated by song, by word, by testimony, in all sorts of ways; but it has to come through personality—not through lips, or eyes, or mind, but through a heart. Only that which has burnt its way deep into the heart will ever make any impression on others.

So then, all gifts, whatever they may be, have to be taken to the Lord Jesus so that natural gifts are not being used without referring them to Him. As a Christian is bought by the cost of the shed blood of the Lord Jesus Christ, so he has no right to self-government or to any reservations at all. Every faculty, every power, every moment is God's. If the cross is simply something to be hung around the neck, if it is merely sentiment or fiction, then let our belonging to Him be fiction too. But if it is true, if redemption is real, then it demands the answer of absolute surrender, for as Paul says, *"therefore* glorify God in your bodies."

So often is sung the lovely hymn of Frances Ridley Havergal which is called her consecration hymn, which starts, "Take my life, and let it be consecrated, Lord, to Thee." It is very interesting, because she begins by saying "Take my life," which is grand. "Take my hands"—splendid; "take my feet"—great! "Take my voice, my lips"—wonderful. "Take my silver and my gold"—unusual but very fine. "Take my love"—that is getting closer, but she is not there yet. "Take my will"—that is nearer still. "Take my self"—now she is there! The last line of the last verse of that consecration hymn hits the punch line: "Take my *self"*—and until Jesus has that, we are breaking this Eighth Commandment: "You shall not steal."

It is so possible to yield to the Lord human talents and gifts, but because He has never been given the self-life, the pathway of fullness has never been entered or proved. The Holy Spirit is the guarantee of my inheritance in Jesus one day in Glory. He it is who comes to take possession of my life, and in return for my absolute surrender of myself, to fill me to overflowing with His life and power.

The Holy Spirit is not an optional extra. There are few people who will become supersaints. He is an indispensable necessity for every child of God. Dr. A. W. Tozer says in one of his books that if the Holy Spirit were to be withdrawn from our churches today, 95 percent of what we do would go on and no one would know any difference—but if the Holy Spirit had been withdrawn from the New Testament church, 95 percent of what they did would stop, and everyone would know the difference.

The Holy Spirit comes primarily to reveal the character of Jesus in me. Where is the fullness of God? In Christ Jesus is all the fullness of God, and I am complete in Him, so that the fullness of God in me is Christ. What is that in terms of life and character?

> But the fruit of the Spirit is love, joy, peace, patience, kindness, goodness, faithfulness, gentleness, self-control; against such things there is no law.
>
> Galatians 5:22, 23

Love, joy, peace: that is our relationship to God.

Patience, kindness, goodness: that is our relationship to other people.

Faithfulness, gentleness, self-control: that is our relationship to ourselves.

God's purpose in giving me His Spirit is to fill me to overflowing with Himself, that it may be never I who live, but Christ who lives in me.

"You shall not steal." Tell me, are all your rights surrendered to Christ? Is His character streaming out through your life as you receive Him in fullness? Maybe you are content to live on a low level of Christian experience, and therefore know nothing of His fullness flooding your heart and life.

The invitation of the Lord Jesus is to those who hunger and thirst after righteousness, for they shall be filled (Matthew 5:6). You may have as much of Him as you desire, but no more, for He meets you on the level of spiritual appetite, and if your heart is hungry for Him, then He will fill you with Himself.

> If any man is thirsty, let him come to Me and drink. He who believes in Me, as the Scripture said, "From his innermost being shall flow rivers of living water."
>
> John 7:37, 38

If the living Lord Jesus is allowed to fill the heart of His child like that, and possess him completely, then he is in no danger of breaking this Commandment. It is indeed no vague Old Testament law that does not matter too much, but a vital New Testament principle to be worked out in life, for He must have all of us, because we can have all of Him through the unhindered infilling of His Holy Spirit.

9

The Ninth Commandment:
WATCH YOUR TONGUE!

You shall not bear false witness against your neighbor.
(Exodus 20:16)

There are two great facts that are of extreme importance in the lives of most people. One is reputation, and the other is character. Reputation is the estimate which other people form of us; character is the embodiment of what we really are. Of course, in fact, reputation ought to be dependent upon character. That this is not so is due to the false idea so many people have of success and greatness, and to the shallow estimate of sin, and to the contempt of the world for godliness. To the child of God, reputation is important. To him, the one thing to be afraid of is sin, and a reputation unsoiled by sin is a precious possession.

Because, you see, the Christian is concerned that his reputation should be built on his character. Now to a non-Christian, to the unbeliever, a reputation is tremendously important: to be unknown, to be little, to be of no consequence, is something to be ashamed of, but the question of character is often not too important.

Now the Lord is tremendously concerned about this question also, and many people who are being condemned by others are guiltless before Him. Why? Because He bases His estimate on what they really are. What one man thinks of another does not matter much.

The Lord Jesus was the supreme example of this. He lost His life at Calvary through the sin of breaking this Ninth Commandment, for the people falsely accused Him (e.g., in Matthew 26:59–61). But God vindicated Him, and God will vindicate all who trust in Him.

In the meantime He guards reputation by this command, for more harm has been done in the world by false testimony concerning other people than will ever be known. Of course, there is a sense in which the Christian must expect it: "Blessed are you when men revile you, and persecute you, and say all kinds of evil against you falsely, on account of me" (Matthew 5:11). But it remains true that the day is coming when the false witness will be punished, and the truth will be vindicated.

Think first about this command itself—what does it mean? "You shall not bear false witness against your neighbor." It simply means speaking the truth concerning your fellowmen. The Third Commandment forbids taking the name of the Lord in vain, which governs our relationship with Him. This Ninth Commandment means that our relationship with other people should be governed by the same principle. God deals with us on the basis of His complete knowledge of what we are, and He is not one bit concerned with the appearances we wish to put on before other people.

> O Lord, Thou has searched me and known me.
> Thou dost know when I sit down and when I rise up;
> Thou dost understand my thought from afar.
>   Psalms 139:1, 2

It is on that basis of God's absolute knowledge of us that He deals with us all.

Now in measure He expects His people to deal with others on the same basis, but our knowledge of them is so limited. But what we say about other people must be true, and nobody is to be helped or hurt by statements made about another which are not in accordance with known truth. The opinions which I produce in the mind of another concerning a third person are to be true. Beyond personal knowledge, no comment should be given. How important this is! The whole social fabric is built upon the testimony of one person concerning another, and if we desire that fabric to be righteous, then what a responsibility exists in relation to this command—speaking the truth, only the known truth, about another.

Now how is this command broken? Perhaps unconsciously, yet how often and in how many ways we break it! First of all by slander, which is a lie invented and spread with intent to do harm. That is the worst form of injury a person can do to another. Compared to one who does this, a gangster is a gentleman, and a murderer is kind, because he ends a life in a moment with a stroke and with little pain. But the man guilty of slander ruins a reputation which may never be regained, and causes lifelong suffering.

Then this law is broken by talebearing, which is repeating a report about a person without careful investigation. Many, many times I have known what it is to suffer with that. To repeat a story which brings discredit and dishonor to another person without making sure of the facts, is breaking this Commandment. How many people, especially Christian people, revel in this, and delight in working havoc by telling tales about others. To excuse the action by saying they believed the report to be true, or that there was no intention to malign, is no justification.

Again, this command is broken by creating false impressions about one person in the mind of another. For instance, Mr. A says to Mr. B, "Have you heard about Brother C?" Mr. B says, "No." To which Mr. A responds, "Oh, well, perhaps the least said the soonest mended"—and the damage has been done. Nothing further may be said at all, but an unfavorable impression is created, and the innuendo has had the effect of lying slander.

This Commandment is also broken by silence. When someone utters a falsity about another and a third person is present who knows that statement to be untrue but, for reason of fear or being disliked, remains quiet, that third person is as guilty of breaking this law as if he had told a lie.

Then it is broken by questioning the motives behind someone's deed or action. A comment is thrown out, such as "Oh, he knows what he is doing—he's on to a good thing." In England we say, "He knows on which side his bread is buttered!" Again the innuendo has been aired.

It is broken by flattery. When something is said concerning a person which is known not to be true, in order to "butter him up," it is to bear false witness.

How easy it is to break this Commandment, isn't it? Can any of us plead not guilty? What a startling revelation it would be if a tape recording could be played of all that every church member has said about his fellow members in one week! What

actions for slander and defamation of character there would be!
The words of the Lord Jesus strongly reinforce this Commandment:

> Do not judge lest you be judged yourselves. For in the
> way you judge, you will be judged; and by your standard
> of measure, it shall be measured to you. And why do you
> look at the speck in your brother's eye, but do not notice
> the log that is in your own eye? Or how can you say to
> your brother, "Let me take the speck out of your eye,"
> and behold, the log is in your own eye? You hypocrite,
> first take the log out of your own eye, and then you will
> see clearly enough to take the speck out of your brother's
> eye.
>
> Matthew 7:1–5

Let us examine that: The Lord does not intend us to be soft, to
have no opinions about anything, for indeed Matthew 7:15
says, "Beware of the false prophets, who come to you in sheep's
clothing, but inwardly are ravenous wolves." Scripture teaches
us there must be discernment, but Jesus says there must never
be condemnation. There must be no attitude of the Pharisee
who thanked God that he was not as other men. There must be
complete absence of the awful sense of superiority that we are
right and other people are wrong. How terribly true that is in
some evangelical circles. If others don't dot their i's and cross
their t's theologically as they do, they won't have any fellowship with anyone. That is Pharisaism in evangelicalism, and it
is of the devil. A person like that is a worse enemy of truth than
a liberal theologian, because he is implying that he has the
truth, and other people, having less, are wrong. A spirit which
is always looking for the worst in others, glad to find their faults
but blind to its own, that is what the Lord Jesus is talking
about. It is a tragedy when a so-called Christian is happy when
he can find another person in the wrong but is absolutely blind,
with shutters drawn, to his own faults and failures.
The Lord Jesus said, "Judge not," because you are inviting
judgment on yourselves. Paul echoes this teaching:

> But you, why do you judge your brother? Or you
> again, why do you regard your brother with contempt?

> For we shall all stand before the judgment-seat of
> God . . . . So then each one of us shall give account of
> himself to God.
>
> Romans 14:10, 12

> For we must all appear before the judgment-seat of
> Christ, that each one may be recompensed for his deeds
> in the body, according to what he has done, whether
> good or bad.
>
> 2 Corinthians 5:10

The Christian faces judgment. Now I know that that judgment is not to determine his eternal destiny, but it is to decide
his qualification for service in heaven. I cannot anticipate the
judgment seat of Christ as a happy party when we receive
prizes and halos, for as Paul says, we must all stand before God
to give an account of the deeds done in the body. Therefore,
judge not lest you be judged yourselves; for you are inviting
judgment upon yourself, and if you judge others you are going
to intensify your own (*see* Matthew 7:2).

Paul again has something pretty strong to say about that:

> Therefore you are without excuse, every man of you
> who passes judgment, for in that you judge another, you
> condemn yourself; for you who judge practice the same
> things . . . . you, therefore, who teach another, do you
> not teach yourself? You who preach that one should not
> steal, do you steal? You who say that one should not
> commit adultery, do you commit adultery? You who
> abhor idols, do you rob temples? You who boast in the
> Law, through your breaking the Law, do you dishonor
> God? For "THE NAME OF GOD IS BLASPHEMED AMONG THE
> GENTILES BECAUSE OF YOU," just as it is written.
>
> Romans 2:1, 21–24

So I have to ask myself, Do I set a high standard upon other
people? Let me be very careful, for one day God will set that
standard upon me. That is what the Lord Jesus said: the standard we have set upon others as the right and norm, but which
we refuse to accept for ourselves, is an attitude of which as
Christians we must be profoundly aware, and beware lest we
fall into the trap of disobedience. How quick we are to pro-

nounce sentence upon another! How quick we are to say we cannot have anything more to do with him, and forget that the judgment we thus pronounce upon him, Jesus will one day pronounce upon us. "Judge not," because we are incapable of it, as the Lord teaches in Matthew 7:3–5, already quoted.

The question I asked myself as I read this portion once in my devotions, I put down in the margin of my Bible, and I share it with you: "Am I willing for other people to judge me, even for God to do so, as I judge them?" Yes, are we really willing to judge ourselves in the same way—to be tough on oneself, but gentle with other people? Let us be honest about this: we must want God's glory and not our own. I would seek to apply this principle to my life by the grace of God, and urge you to do the same: Be tough on yourself, but be gentle with others.

Some people are so concerned, so they say, about "defending the faith." This is sometimes not true, for so often the truth is not faced in their own lives. Those who are the most stalwart defenders of the truth are many times people who refuse to accept the truth in their own lives. We must be very careful regarding our judgment and criticism of other people, for in thus judging them we find ourselves judged.

That is how this Commandment is broken—but how ever can it be kept? The apostle James has a lot to say about it. This half brother of the Lord Jesus had learned much from Him. At first he was very skeptical, but in his letter he amplifies and repeats portions of the Sermon on the Mount many times. There are more quotations from that section of the Lord's teaching in the Epistle of James than in any other letter in the Bible, though often Paul is on the same track in Romans 13.

> For we all stumble in many ways. If any one does not stumble in what he says, he is a perfect man, able to bridle the whole body as well. Now if we put the bits into the horses' mouths so that they may obey us, we direct their entire body as well . . . . So also the tongue is a small part of the body, and yet it boasts of great things. Behold, how great a forest is set aflame by such a small fire! And the tongue is a fire, the very world of iniquity; the tongue is set among our members as that which defiles the entire body, and sets on fire the course of our life, and is set on fire by hell . . . . no one can

tame the tongue; it is a restless evil and full of deadly
poison. With it we bless our Lord and Father; and with it
we curse men, who have been made in the likeness of
God; from the same mouth come both blessing and cursing. My brethren, these things ought not to be this way.

James 3:2–10

What a lot James has to say about the tongue! Often a doctor
can look at his patient's tongue and be helped in his diagnosis.
Will you let the Lord Jesus see your tongue? James has shown
how the tongue directs our lives just as a bit directs a horse, and
the rudder directs a great ship. What a wonderful thing the
tongue can be in direction! What a power for good it can be!

Years ago the friend who led me to Christ took me out to
lunch in London. I had been a Christian only a short time and
was busy in Christian work. I told him throughout the lunch
about the number of people I had spoken to about Christ and
how busy I was in the Lord's work, but he did not seem to be
the least impressed! He listened, but as I did not seem to be
getting it over to him, I stopped speaking, and at the end of the
lunch he said to me, "Excuse me one moment; I think the waiter
who served our lunch needs to hear about Jesus." He crossed
the restaurant floor, spoke to the waiter about Christ, gave him
a New Testament, and returned to his seat. I felt about an inch
high!

Years later an African brother, William Ngenda, came to
preach at Moody Church with Ugandan Bishop Festo
Kivengere, who has since fled his native land. I had known
these two great men of God for some years, as they had been
from time to time in Britain. It was early in January, and I said
to William that we had taken as our year's verse at the church
the words "Sir, we would see Jesus." When he got up to speak
he said, "Your pastor has told me your year verse, which is a
very good one. But remember, if you would see Jesus, He must
first see you." Then he preached one of the most remarkable
sermons, comparing Jehu in the Old Testament—who rode
furiously and said, "Come see my zeal for the Lord!"—with the
woman of Samaria who said to the people of her village,
"Come, see a Man who told me all things ever I did!"

What a power the tongue can be for good!

But notice it not only directs, it damages: "So also the tongue is a small part of the body, and yet it boasts of great things. Behold, how great a forest is set aflame by such a small fire! And the tongue is a fire . . . . no one can tame the tongue; it is a restless evil and full of deadly poison" (James 3:5, 6, 8).

At the supper table a man said to his wife, "Honey, I am off to the deacons' meeting tonight, and I'm going to give them all a piece of my mind. Pray for me." It was not he who needed praying for, it was the people who were to be at the receiving end of his tongue! How very strange that we have ever come to think that Christian maturity is shown by the ability to speak our minds, whereas it is really expressed in controlling our tongues.

The tongue directs, it damages, and it dispenses:

> Does a fountain send out from the same opening both fresh and bitter water? Can a fig tree, my brethren, produce olives, or a vine produce figs? Neither can salt water produce fresh . . . . From the same mouth come both blessing and cursing. My brethren, these things ought not to be this way.
>
> James 3:11, 12, 10

Well, I am still left to answer the question of how to keep the Commandment. Maybe you sense the conviction of the Spirit of God, because this is exactly how we behave and what we do. So turn now to Jesus for the answer, so stern in His rebuke, so tender in His forgiving love. Remember first of all that no one suffered at the hands of other people so much as He did in the breaking of this law. What wonderful words Peter wrote: "While being reviled, He did not revile in return; while suffering, He uttered no threats, but kept entrusting Himself to Him who judges righteously" (1 Peter 2:23).

It is such a comfort to know when we are maligned that Jesus understands, and such a challenge to think how He reacted.

In her book *Gold by Moonlight,* Amy Carmichael tells the story of a pastor who had been viciously slandered by gossip about his character, gossip that was completely unfounded and untrue. He could have left and gone to another church, but he chose to ride it out. One day at Sunday School, his small daughter was asked after the class by her teacher, "Tell me, how has all this gossip about your father reacted on him?" And the girl replied, "It has made it absolutely impossible for my dad to say an unkind word about anybody."

That is victory. Jesus understands, and it is a precious thing to be able to leave our case in His hands.

Of course, the Lord forgives us this particular sin when we repent and confess it to Him, as He does all other sins, because He died for this and His blood was shed to cleanse us from it. There is only one sin He does not forgive, and that is the sin that we refuse to confess. If I refuse to confess and forsake sin, I become involved in the judgment of it. That is only reasonable. The Lord does not forgive unconfessed sin, but "if we confess our sins, He is faithful and righteous to forgive us our sins and to cleanse us from all unrighteousness" (1 John 1:9). The *one* sin He can never forgive is blasphemy against the Holy Spirit (Matthew 12:31). Bearing false witness against the Holy Spirit is the unforgivable sin. If we want to know what that means, it is the constant resistance to His voice and His claim upon us. That is the unforgivable sin. To go on resisting the Holy Spirit, to refuse to bend before His authority, is to head for judgment.

Ah, Jesus lives to deliver us from this sin of bearing false witness as from every other. To yield to Christ is to possess His Spirit in our hearts, and the first fruit of the Spirit is love. Love becomes the motive and the relationship of every contact with people, because love and truth are inseparable partners. How we need to pray the language of the Psalmist: "Set a guard, O Lord, over my mouth;/Keep watch over the door of my lips" (Psalms 141:3).

The truth is that the source of the trouble is about twelve inches lower than our lips, in the heart, for as a man thinks within himself, so he is (Proverbs 23:7). It is what comes out of a man that defiles him (Matthew 15:11), and the control of *His* Spirit over *my* spirit is the only way of deliverance. I cannot have a tamed tongue until my heart is under Holy Spirit control.

In one of my pastorates, during a difficult period, at a midweek service I wrote on a blackboard three big letters: M E F. That stood for Mutual Encouragement Fellowship. I said to the people, "How many of you would like to join MEF to encourage one another in the Lord? I will give you the terms of membership. And I wrote vertically, *THINK. T* stood for "Is it True?" *H,* "Will it Help?" *I,* "Is it Inspiring?" *N,* "Is it Necessary?" *K,* "Is it Kind?'' If what I am about to say does not pass all those tests, I will keep my mouth shut!

If these principles were applied, many churches would be a long way on the road to spiritual revival.

Surely the love of God shed abroad in your heart is the answer, but you must cooperate and show the Lord that you mean business. No *man* can tame the tongue, but THINK—think before you speak, and as the Lord controls thought and speech, what an atmosphere of love would rapidly spread! How this control would transform your next morning coffee hour, and purify your next telephone conversation! For the Lord alone can make a backbiting tongue kind, and a lying tongue truthful. He can make a passionate, explosive tongue gentle. He alone can liberate love in your life, and diffuse an atmosphere of tender care for other people, so you will begin to take fire with Holy Spirit life and love and liberty.

10

The Tenth Commandment:

WATCH YOUR DESIRES!

You shall not covet your neighbor's house; you shall not covet your neighbor's wife or his male servant or his female servant or his ox or his donkey or anything that belongs to your neighbor. (Exodus 20:17)

This commandment, above all others, is at the root of everything that governs the life of those who would know God and who would be used by Him: "You shall not covet." Maybe you have read through the other nine, and have somehow escaped their challenge. You are still left with a consciousness that perhaps you have not done so badly, and have not sinned so greatly after all.

I find that it is absolutely impossible to stand in the light of this last command and remain guiltless. Do you remember that it was this Commandment that brought Saul of Tarsus to his knees? That self-righteous Pharisee, after thirty years of Christian experience, reviewing his old life as a Hebrew, a Jew, described it "as to the righteousness which is in the Law, found blameless" (Philippians 3:6). But when he faced this final command, hear what he says in Romans 7:

> What shall we say then? Is the Law sin? May it never be! On the contrary, I would not have come to know sin except through the Law; for I would not have known about coveting if the Law had not said, "You shall not covet." But sin, taking opportunity through the commandment produced in me coveting of every kind; for apart from the Law sin is dead. And I was once alive apart from the Law; but when the commandment came, sin became alive, and I died; and this commandment, which was to result in life, proved to result in death for

me; for sin, taking opportunity through the commandment, deceived me, and through it killed me.
                                                    Romans 7:7–11

Paul is saying that it is the Law which instructs us in right
behavior, and if we throw over God's law and His Commandments, we end up behaving like animals. The Law provokes us
to rebellion. It is a strange thing, but the very fact that a person
is forbidden to do something arouses in him the desire to do it,
which is what Paul is talking about. The very Commandment
which promised life proved to be death, because there is evil
inside all of us that uses every means it can to drag us into sin.
There are many attractive things that we must not do, and the
Law just plays into their hands, and we end up by doing them.
That is why it is never enough to tell people to live un-
selfishly; they need to be introduced to the Lord Jesus Christ if
they are to find an answer.

It is true that the teaching of this Tenth Commandment
shows us what sin really is, and brings us to repentance and
dedication of life to Christ for His use. You see, it is only the
utterly surrendered life which is set free from the sin of coveting.

Now let us follow the same course of analyzing this Commandment as we have the others, looking at it first of all as it
stands in the Old Testament. At once you notice, if you are
seriously studying, a very clear distinction between this law
and all the others. To disobey the others involves detection by
other people at once, but it is possible to disobey this one and
for no other person to know about it. Of course, sooner or later,
coveting results in outward action, and therefore how tremendously solemn it is that this word deals with the mind and the
inner life of every person. "You shall not covet" goes beyond
and deeper than action, right deep down to the source, and
challenges us with a hidden resolve of our mind, our heart, and
will, that there we should set up the sovereignty of God to
ensure that every desire might be under His control.

So this command not only deals with relationships with other
people as do the previous three, but it puts every relationship
in its right context in relation to God, showing that God has to
strike at the root of every desire that is contrary to His will if
this law is to remain unbroken. Unsatisfied desires poison

every relationship of life, and the Lord says, "You shall not covet."

Now what is coveting? It means eagerly to desire what belongs to another, to set the heart on something; to "pant after something" would be the literal translation. It works like this: The eyes look upon an object; the mind admires it; the will goes over to it; and the body moves in to possess it. That is coveting. Of course it is assumed that the desire is illegitimate. You may admire your friend's car and then perhaps buy one like it, but that is not coveting. But if you were to take his car, then you have coveted! If you look at it, admire it, and your will desires it, and the body moves over to possess it, then you step into the driver's seat, turn the key to start the engine, and you are off, that is coveting which has led to action—in fact, to stealing.

It is not wrong to desire a wife, but it is wrong to desire the wife of another man. The whole force of this Commandment is that you shall not covet your neighbor's house, his wife, his servants, his ox or his ass (that is, his car!), or his lawnmower, or anything else that is his. Doesn't this go right down and search out to the very depths of our desires?

That is the command as it stands: You shall not covet anything that belongs to your neighbor. Now surely this shows us what the human heart is like, for we are all made in the same mold (some of us may be moldier than others), but this is the true condition of the human heart, for the fact that sin is present in us all is revealed by the desire to possess something that is forbidden.

You will recall this is exactly how sin entered the human race. In Genesis 3:6 it is recorded that when Eve "saw that the tree was good for food, and that it was a delight to the eyes, and that the tree was desirable to make one wise, she took from its fruit and ate; and she gave also to her husband with her, and he ate."

Observe the verbs in that verse: she *saw*, she *delighted*, she *desired*, she *took*, she *ate*, she *gave*. That is coveting.

This sin would appear to begin with the eyes, but it does not; it goes further back than that. To see the root of it, read a familiar story. People say, "What a fuss God made about an apple!" There is nothing in the Bible about an apple. That is pure fiction. But see how sin entered into the human experience:

Now the serpent was more crafty than any beast of the field which the Lord God had made. And he said to the woman, "Indeed, has God said, 'You shall not eat from any tree of the garden'?" [implying, Can your Creator be so unkind as that?] And the woman said to the serpent [here was her mistake, having conversation with the devil], "From the fruit of the trees of the garden we may eat; but from the fruit of the tree which is in the middle of the garden, God has said, 'You shall not eat from it or touch it, lest you die.' "

Genesis 3:1–3

Now that is not true, for that is not what the Lord had said to Adam and Eve. He said, "From any tree of the garden you may eat freely; but from the tree of the knowledge of good and evil you shall not eat, for in the day that you eat from it you shall surely die" (Genesis 2:16, 17).

As Eve discussed the matter with the serpent, her doubts all began when he questioned God's word: "Has God said . . . ?" And she listened to him. When he spoke he used the word *Elohim* (the Mighty God), implying, "Has your Mighty God said this? Can He be so unkind?" Throughout the previous chapter, when the Lord was giving His promises and His covenant to Adam, He spoke of Himself as Jehovah, the covenant-keeping God, the One who never breaks a promise. But Satan was clever enough to take her right off covenant ground and say, "Has Elohim said . . . ?" And she went right along with him: "Yes, Elohim has said . . . ."

Eve, that's done it—you have forsaken the covenant promises of God, and you have retreated from covenant ground. You are meeting the devil on a lower level. You have already forgotten the promise and covenant of your God Jehovah, who said to you, "You may freely eat of every tree," while you said to the devil that the Lord told you that you may eat from the fruit of the trees of the garden. Not only was Eve doubting God's word, but she diluted His word and minimized His provision. He used the word *freely,* while she said, "Well, God told us we may eat of the trees."

She even went further, because she exaggerated the Lord's prohibition. He had said, "From the tree of the knowledge of good and evil you shall not eat . . . ." Eve said, "From the fruit of the tree which is in the middle of the garden, God has said, 'You shall not eat from it or touch it . . . .' " The Lord had said nothing about touching the tree, only about taking and eating from it. Merely to touch something does not make one covet it necessarily, but to take and eat a fruit which is forbidden is the complete act.

Finally she weakened His penalty, for the Lord said, "You shall die," while Eve said, "We might die." In other words, the connection between disobedience and penalty is not certain. So you see, the devil goes a yard further and says to her, "You surely shall not die!" (verse 4): Go ahead and disobey! You can get away with it.

Finally we read (verse 6), "When the woman saw that the tree was good for food . . . ." So coveting did not begin with looking. It began with listening to the devil, who weakened her hold upon God and His word. He made her forget the promise of the covenant-keeping God, then made her minimize His grace, exaggerate His prohibition, and weaken His penalty, until she agreed with Satan that He was not fair after all, and finally when she saw, she took.

That tells me a lot: it tells me that a man who soaks his life in prayer and in the Word of God is always ready with an answer for the devil. Thank Him that He sent the second Adam, the Lord Jesus Christ, who confronted face to face the greatest rebel in the universe with the words "It is written . . ." (*see* Matthew 4:1–11).

The Son of God was ready with an answer to the devil from the authoritative Word of God, and the weakest and most insignificant child of God has exactly the same mighty weapon, the sword of the Spirit, which is the Word of God (Ephesians 6:17).

This is the answer to coveting. It does not begin with the eye, though it is weakened because all the senses are weakened when we do not rest in His word or draw upon His promises and His power to use them to counter every attack of the Adversary. Satan is easier to reject than eject. He is harder to deal with if he has taken you halfway than if you catch him at the very beginning. If you want to be delivered from unholy desires, there is only one secret: cling to a holy God, to the au-

thority of His Word, and to the surety of His promises. Cast
yourself upon Him and His power, and He has strength to
change those desires and make them holy.

> Let no one say when he is tempted, "I am being temp-
> ted by God"; for God cannot be tempted by evil, and He
> Himself does not tempt any one. But each one is tempted
> when he is carried away and enticed by his own lust.
>
> James 1:13, 14

"Carried away" is the inward combustible material in us all;
"enticed" is the output of fascination and attraction, for James
continues: "Then when lust has conceived, it gives birth to sin;
and when sin is accomplished, it brings forth death" (verse 15).

Do you see the process? The dawn of human failure, the
incoming of sin and evil, is as up to date as the morning paper.
Eve saw, she delighted, she desired, she took, she ate and she
passed on the forbidden fruit. It need never have happened if,
when Satan came at her and said, "Elohim . . . ," Eve had
replied, "Oh, no, I do not answer you in His name, but in the
name of my Lord Jehovah." For the Lord had given Adam and
Eve His covenant and His promise in the name of Jehovah, but
Satan took her off that ground, and beat her.

This Tenth Commandment, therefore, touches every aspect
of life. It touches the personal life because covetousness makes
it impossible to be a Christian. I hope you realize that, for it
does. What is the fruit of the Spirit outlined in Galatians 5:22,
23? "Love, joy, peace"—my relationship to God; "patience,
kindness, goodness"—my relationship to other people; "faithfulness, gentleness, self-control"—my relationship to myself.

If you list these qualities vertically, you find that when the
law of covetousness is broken, in the place of love there is hate;
instead of joy there is sorrow; instead of peace there is unrest;
instead of long-suffering there is impatience; instead of kindness there is cruelty; instead of goodness there is selfishness;
instead of faithfulness there is infidelity; instead of gentleness
there is arrogance; instead of self-control there are self-
assurance and self-assertiveness.

Down the original column one can write: "This is the Christ-
life." Across the second column can be written: "This is the self-

life." When a person covets, in the place of the glorious fruit of the Christ-life come up all the evil growth of the self-life. But to those who have fallen into the sin of coveting, and have found this to be true, there is a word of glorious promise from the prophetic Scripture, taken rather out of context, but nevertheless a truth to be claimed: "*Instead of* the thorn bush the cypress will come up;/And *instead of* the nettle the myrtle will come up . . ." (Isaiah 55:13, *italics added*).

Underline those words in your heart and read it again. As has been said before, God is never in the self-improvement plan but always in the Christ-replacement plan, and He is the opposite to everything that we are. The opposite to all we are by nature is in Christ, and if Christ is in us by faith, then He alone is the answer to covetousness. He touches our personal life, and He touches our social life too, because unholy desire is at the root of murder, robbery, adultery, and all the dire ills and sins of modern society. All these Commandments are broken sooner or later when we covet. The awful sin of false witness is often inspired by the jealousy of the success of another.

But most serious of all, this command just makes nonsense of our relationship to the Lord Jesus. If a Christian covets, he is telling Him plainly that his heart is completely out of harmony with Him, and he is dissatisfied with Him. A man who loves the Lord will not covet anything except what God supplies: "Delight yourself in the Lord;/And He will give you the desires of your heart" (Psalms 37:4).

Every desire with no exceptions? Yes, every desire—for if you delight in the Lord Jesus your one desire will be only His will for you, and therefore you will truly be able to say that Jesus satisfies.

Now look at the command as Jesus enforced it. Nothing could be clearer or more emphatic. Do not think that He brings you under the Law, therefore you are finished with the Law in this new dispensation. That is nonsense. This is not Old Testament truth; it is New Testament reality empowered in us by God's Holy Spirit.

> Beware, and be on your guard against every form of greed [covetousness]; for not even when one has an abundance does his life consist of his possessions.
> Luke 12:15

> Do not lay up for yourselves treasures upon earth,
> where moth and rust destroy, and where thieves break in
> and steal; but lay up for yourselves treasures in heaven,
> where neither moth nor rust destroys, and where thieves
> do not break in or steal; for where your treasure is, there
> will your heart be also . . . . You cannot serve God and
> Mammon.
>
> Matthew 6:19–21, 24

> Seek first [first in order of priority, first in order of
> desire] His kingdom and His righteousness; and all these
> things shall be added to you.
>
> Matthew 6:33

What tremendous words those are! How they expose real covetousness, the search after something which, in the restless energy of desire, is absolutely out of God's will. It is the fever which makes the face of a man flushed and his nerves throb in the desire of possession, and the final wages of it is death. To desire anything beyond God's will is to desire something which will ultimately destroy us unless that desire is quenched.

The most subtle and serious thing has yet to be said. Did you ever realize that it is coveting which silences the missionary call? It cripples missionary support. It makes Christian living impossible, because the child of God covets himself and desires only self-preservation. To listen to the questions which some candidates ask mission boards amazes me, and I have had the privilege of serving on several. They go like this (this is the candidate speaking):

Would you mind telling us what the social security will be? How long have we to serve before we earn a right to part of it?

We are not quite sure if we can take the tropical climate, and after all, we can not know until we get into one; would you mind our being there for a few months and trying it out?

What is going to happen about our children's education? Are we quite sure they will be well looked after?

I wonder what the apostle Paul would have thought of that! He said, "I count not my life dear to me." The self-preservation of a life that has never given way to the spirit of self-sacrifice, which is at the root of living for the Lord Jesus, is covetousness—snatching it for oneself.

Perhaps you have lived long enough to know that no amount

of getting out of God's will can ever be gain; it is always loss, and the hardest thing for any of us to face is to deny our right to ourselves. But Jesus said, "If any one wishes to come after Me, let him deny himself, and take up his cross, and follow Me. For whoever wishes to save his life shall lose it; but whoever loses his life for My sake shall find it" (Matthew 16:24, 25).

Can you sign your name to those terms of discipleship? Your sin of coveting may have escaped the notice of other people, but it has not escaped the notice of the Lord, and there are some people languishing in Christian service—just riding it out, sitting on a pew, occupying a seat on Sunday, contributing a little to the church and missionary program, going to services and often criticizing the preacher because they think he is not sound—and they are coveting. They covet their money, their right to themselves, their time and service, and that is why only a trickle of recruits get out to serving the Lord, both overseas and in the home ministry. Young people claim a right to dictate their own life pattern; parents are reluctant to let their young folk loose to seek the will of God, and hold on to them so that they can settle near at home, work in the family business, follow their own ambitious plans for them, which may be wide of the mark of God's will for them. Stop coveting that which belongs and those who belong to the Lord, and allow Him the right to do what He wills with His own!

Coveting is to set the heart on that which belongs to another, and the life of every Christian belongs to the Lord Jesus, for He has purchased it. Have you ever said to Him, "Thine, Lord, would I be"?

Do I covet my sons, my daughters, my family, for my old age or for my own desires? Do these things matter to me more so that in my declining years I will have enough to live on and can end my days comfortably so that all will be well *for me?* Do I want to feather my nest, or am I really prepared to accept Christ's terms of discipleship?

There is one new Commandment which fulfills all the other ten:

A new commandment I give to you, that you love one another, even as I have loved you, that you also love one another. By this all men will know that you are My disciples, if you have love for one another.

John 13:34, 35

He who has My commandments and keeps them, he it
is who loves Me; and he who loves Me shall be loved by
My Father, and I will love him, and will disclose Myself
to him . . . . If anyone loves Me, he will keep My word;
and My Father will love him, and We will come to him,
and make Our abode with him.

John 14:21, 23

If you keep My commandments, you will abide in My
love; just as I have kept My Father's commandments, and
abide in His love . . . . This is My commandment, that
you love one another, just as I have loved you. Greater
love has no one than this, that one lay down his life for
his friends. You are My friends, if you do what I command you.

John 15:10, 12–14

Jesus came to fulfill every command, and having loved His
own, He loved them to the end, and thus all the requirements of
His law were met by His life, because His every motive was
love. He did not set aside any of the Commandments. He established them all that in the mighty force of His love to the heart
of His people He would set up His kingdom of love in them by
His Holy Spirit.

Paul says love is the fulfillment of the Law. Of course—for if I
love the Lord Jesus I find no room for other gods. If I love Him
there will be no graven image in my life. If I love Him, I hallow
His name. If I love the Lord, then the Lord's day is a.sheer
delight. If I love God supremely I learn always to love my parents and to honor them. If I love Him, there will be no thought
of murder. If I love Jesus, there will be no thought of unchastity
or unfaithfulness to husband or wife. If I love Him supremely, I
cannot possibly steal. If I love Him with all my heart, I would
never, never betray someone else's character. If I love God
above all, I would never think of coveting.

You may say that is sinless perfection. No, it is the life of
Jesus in me. Everything else is total corruption. How wonderful
that He comes into the arena of our hearts, which have broken
every one of these Ten Commandments—I have, haven't you?
Is there any one of these ten about which you can say "Not
guilty"? I know there is not. Each and every one of us has
broken all ten of them at some time in our lives, and the Lord

steps into that arena of filth and sets up His life of love and holiness. When that happens, love is lavish—nay, imprudent! Love takes the precious ointment and pours it out without regard to the cost. Love goes the second mile. Love sweeps through every boundary of creed and race and color. Love does not care about criticism if it can only serve others. Love carries a message of hope to every dark corner of the world. Love thinks of other people, and love forgets itself.

> Love is patient, love is kind, and is not jealous; love does not brag and is not arrogant, does not act unbecomingly; it does not seek its own, it is not provoked, does not take into account a wrong suffered, does not rejoice in unrighteousness, but rejoices with the truth; bears all things, believes all things, hopes all things, endures all things. Love never fails . . . .
>
> 1 Corinthians 13:4–8

But have you ever read the above verses replacing the word *love* with *Jesus;* "Jesus is patient, Jesus is kind, and is not jealous; Jesus does not brag and is not arrogant, does not act unbecomingly . . ."?

Further, would you be prepared to put *your* name there: "Bill [George, Mary, Jean] is patient, kind, not jealous . . ."?

That is the miracle of the Christian faith, imparting the love of Jesus to each of his children and then through them to others. How desperately you and I need a new baptism of love! The supreme evidence of love is that the Lord Jesus was prepared to take the blame that was due to others, and that is what He did on the cross. The death of Christ saves me from the penalty of what I do; the risen life of Christ saves me from the power of what I am.

The Lord Jesus said, "I lay down My life that I may take it again" (John 10:17), and that principle becomes ours as we say to Him, "Lord, I lay down my life that I may take it again." The life you so covetously sought to preserve and grasp to yourself is now handed back to its rightful Owner, so that you can look into His face and say with grateful heart, "Lord Jesus, I am all Yours for Your use, any time, anywhere, anyhow, with no reservations." Then, and only then, you can take it again, but now not your life but His to live through.

11

THE VICTORY OF LOVE

And day by day the Lord added to their number those
whom he was saving. (Acts 2:47 NEB)

The implications of all that has been said so far when applied
to personal life are immense—indeed, revolutionary. But not
only so, for if they are allowed to permeate through the life of
the Church, first of all at local level and then in increasing areas
of impact, I believe with all my heart that they would be the key
that unlocks the door to release Holy Spirit revival, which is so
urgently needed. Therefore in the concluding chapter of this
book I wish to review the whole by a consideration of this vital
factor.

Look again at the text at the head of the chapter. Here is
something that the Lord did. This is not a matter of additions to
a church roll or a membership drive, but something that in the
exercise of His sovereign will, the Lord effected. And He did it
because conditions within the Church were such that they
called forth such a demonstration of His power. Indeed they are
nothing less than the fulfillment of the promise of John 14:12:
"Truly, truly, I say to you, he who believes in Me, the works
that I do shall he do also; and greater works than these shall he
do; because I go to the Father."

The greater works that the Lord promised there are not the
raising of a few more Lazaruses or the healing of a few more
sick people, but the transforming of entire lives through the
indwelling might of the Spirit of God, with the resultant mul-
tiplication in the Church. What a victory!

Eagerly, almost wistfully, we bend our will and open our

heart to the ministry of the Holy Spirit today and cry, "O God, do it again! Show us how it can happen, and why it has not happened, and give us grace to remedy the wrong."

This chapter has witnessed the birth of the most amazing society the world has ever known. Without directorate, with no committees and no talented leadership, composed in the main of unschooled and unlettered men, without financial resources and born amidst hostile people who could command vast material power which might easily be enough to crush it. They had little doctrine, but that followed to explain their experience; alas that so often the Church today has much doctrine but so little experience to explain!

Yet around this society were centered all the hopes of God— the Father, the Son, and the Holy Spirit—for through it His purposes for the world were to be fulfilled. For the formation of it, He had given Himself. Now He had come to live in the heart of every member of it, that He might direct, control, and guide.

If His hopes were not to be disappointed, and His purposes not to be frustrated, what do you consider must be the one quality the Church must possess? If it is really to be a power in the world, to influence and even shape the future course of world history, what must it have above everything else? Let us answer that question by asking another: What quality was lacking in the lives of those through whom God had been dealing to fulfill His purpose in Old Testament days? Where did these men fail? Listen to the answer of the Lord Jesus in Matthew 22:35–40:

> And one of them, a lawyer, asked Him a question, testing Him, "Teacher, which is the great commandment in the Law?"
> And He said to him, " 'You shall love the Lord your God with all your heart, and with all your soul, and with all your mind.' This is the great and foremost commandment. And a second is like it, 'You shall love your neighbor as yourself.' On these two commandments depend the whole Law and the Prophets."

There was the point of breakdown: *love*. But listen to the answer in the New Testament:

I do not ask in behalf of these alone, but for those also who believe in Me through their word; that they may all be one; even as Thou, Father, art in Me, and I in Thee, that they also may be in Us; that the world may believe that Thou didst send Me. And the glory which Thou hast given Me I have given to them; that they may be one, just as We are one; I in them, and Thou in Me, that they may be perfected in unity, that the world may know that Thou didst send Me, and didst love them, even as Thou didst love Me.

John 17:20–23

Jesus said to Simon Peter, "Simon, son of John, do you love Me more than these?" . . . He said to him again a second time, "Simon, son of John, do you love Me?" . . . He said to him the third time, "Simon, son of John, do you love Me?"

John 21:15–17

If I speak with the tongues of men and of angels, but do not have love, I have become a noisy gong or a clanging cymbal.

1 Corinthians 13:1

And so, as those who have been chosen of God, holy and beloved, put on a heart of compassion, kindness, humility, gentleness and patience; bearing with one another, and forgiving each other, whoever has a complaint against any one; just as the Lord forgave you, so also should you. And beyond all these things put on love, which is the perfect bond of unity.

Colossians 3:12–14

Now for this very reason also, applying all diligence, in your faith supply moral excellence . . . and in your godliness, brotherly kindness, and in your brotherly kindness, Christian love.

2 Peter 1:5, 7

Beloved, let us love one another, for love is from God; and every one who loves is born of God and knows God . . . . Beloved, if God so loved us, we also ought to

love one another . . . . We love, because He first loved
us. If some one says, "I love God," and hates his brother,
he is a liar; for the one who does not love his brother
whom he has seen, cannot love God whom he has not
seen.

                                                    1 John 4:7, 11, 19, 20

Yes, Pentecost has marked the entrance into the world of
something never before known. The Church is to confront
every generation with the love of God which "has been poured
out within our hearts through the Holy Spirit who was given to
us" (Romans 5:5).

The influential church—so often regarded as such because of
the kind of people who attend, or because of money at its
disposal—is in fact the church governed not by intellectual ability, but by Holy Spirit love in the heart of every believing
member. The gifts of the Holy Spirit certainly have their place,
but love is the new dynamic which the world is to feel.

This love is not a patronizing affection, or a mere courtesy or
affability, but the word that is used in John 3:16: "For God so
loved the world . . . ." The love of God is a love which hurts,
which costs, which gives all. If you want to see it in all its
power, look at the cross, and behold the Son of God suffering
and dying for a world of sinners.

Now it is this which led to Holy Spirit love being liberated at
Pentecost to be the greatest factor in evangelism through all
Church history. Here in Acts 2 you see it in operation in the
Church, and you see the effect of it upon the world. This is
highlighted in three words which we will consider together:
fellowship (verse 42), *fear* (a sense of awe, verse 43), and *favor*
(verse 47).

See, therefore, the characteristics of the love-filled Church as
they meet in fellowship—first, their devotion: "And they were
continually devoting themselves to the apostles' teaching and to
fellowship, to the breaking of bread and to prayer" (verse 42).

Here is demonstrated a love for the Word of God, as they
returned to it again and again. These early disciples did not
regard it as something merely to be discussed and criticized but
as something which shattered them by its absolute authority.

Resulting from this there was a love for one another in a
selfless fellowship:

And all those who had believed were together, and
had all things in common; and they began selling their
property and possessions, and were sharing them with
all, as anyone might have need. And day by day continuing with one mind in the temple, and breaking bread
from house to house, they were taking their meals together with gladness and sincerity of heart . . . .

Acts 2: 44–46

Here is love for the Lord demonstrated in breaking of bread
from house to house. Note, *not* in a church building but from
house to house. House groups are nothing new. The Church
gets into trouble when she builds walls and sets up a kind of
defensive mechanism, whereas it should always be out where
the action is. The only reason for the Church's existence on
earth is mission.

Here is a love for prayer: they were really together in the early
Church, showing a oneness in every area of their lives, spiritually and socially.

Here is the victory of love in the Church—but fellowship,
koinonia, is not merely sentiment. It is first devotion, but it is
also discipline.

Listen to a wonderful Old Testament illustration of both devotion and discipline:

For day by day men came to David to help him, until
there was a great army like the army of God . . . . All
these, being men of war, who could draw up in battle
formation ["that could keep rank," in the King James
Version], came to Hebron with a perfect heart, to make
David king over all Israel; and all the rest also of Israel
were of one mind to make David king.

1 Chronicles 12:22, 38

Day by day men collected around David until there were no
less than 340,822 of them, devoted to him, who had learned to
"keep rank." And that must be true if the Lord Jesus is to be our
King: As soldiers in an army, we have to learn to keep rank.

That means we cannot always do as we like, or just what we
would do if we were on our own. It means that our own opinions, views, and preferences have sometimes to be given up in

order to keep rank. Some Christians never realize that, and want to be individualists all the time, and if their views are not accepted they step out of rank. It is Dr. Vance Havner who said in my hearing, "When the tide is out, every little shrimp has its own puddle. But when the tide comes in . . . !"

We cannot always agree, but we can always agree to disagree agreeably! People who can be relied on only when everything goes according to their liking will soon find they are not being taken seriously in the army and their place is being filled by others who are more reliable. Fellowship in the Church corrects exaggerated ideas of one's own importance. Opinions and preferences, which are often due to prejudice, are removed as they are submitted to the discipline of fellowship.

Is there not an essential connection, and indeed an inevitable outflow, between the fact that David's men gathered day by day, and then learned to keep rank? The one is the outcome of the other. Here, in Acts 2, the Lord is gathering His Church together day by day, and He has been doing that for the past nearly two thousand years. May He see the Church of this day learning to "keep rank" and ceasing from fragmentation.

That is the victory of love outlined in Acts 2:42–47: love for His Word, love for one another, love for the Lord. May the Lord give us that today!

But the fact is, the Church has never been so fragmented as it is now. Some people take the extreme reformed Calvinistic position which cuts the nerve of all evangelism. Others take the extreme charismatic position which insists on speaking in tongues as evidence of the baptism of the Holy Spirit, which is totally unbiblical. Some say we must be independent of all denominations. Others prefer to serve within denominations and make their witness there. Some hold to the inerrancy of the Word of God. Others prefer to call it infallibility. Some hold to the pretribulation rapture of the Church. Others take the amillennial position. And about all these issues, and many others, there is a furious civil war. Why cannot truth be held in balance, and love prevail?

Thank God for the great truths of Calvin, and all the doctrines that are so essential to our faith. Thank the Lord also for the tremendous release of Holy Spirit life and power through the emphasis of the charismatic movement. Of course there are counterfeits in both of these areas, but wherever there is coun-

terfeit there is also reality. Why then should we discard, or at
least back off from, reality because of counterfeit? The Word of
God without the Spirit of God is dead. An experience of the
Spirit of God without being based on the Word of God is
dangerous. But ally solid doctrine to Holy Spirit life and you
have dynamite! There is nothing more needed in the Church
today than that. [This subject is dealt with more fully in the
author's book on First Corinthians, *The Royal Route to Heaven.*]

My dear reader, we may hold different views in many matters
on the Word of God which all evangelicals realize are open to
alternative interpretation, but we just have no right whatever to
refuse to show love and fellowship with those who disagree
with us and yet are members of His body and know the reality
of Holy Spirit life and love.

Now will you notice the consequences upon the world of
such fellowship, which were twofold: something happened on
earth, and something happened in heaven. "Everyone kept
feeling a sense of awe" (verse 43), or as the King James Version
puts it, "fear came upon every soul." Here is a Church to be
feared! That sense of awe and conviction which grips the heart
of an unbeliever in the presence of a Holy Spirit-filled commu-
nity. Oh, that this would meet and confront the stranger who
enters the doors of our churches! That sense of the presence of
the Lord which forbids anything of unreality in our worship,
making people almost afraid to come inside lest they get con-
verted.

> And great fear came upon the whole church, and upon
> all who heard of these things. And at the hands of the
> apostles many signs and wonders were taking place
> among the people . . . . But none of the rest dared to
> associate with them; however, the people held them in
> high esteem.
>
> Acts 5:11–13

I well remember when I was a young man, saved but living
far from the Lord at the time, something drew me Sunday by
Sunday to the Central Hall, Westminster in London. The big
building would be packed with some 3,000 people to listen to
an elderly man, Dr. Dinsdale Young. His hair was white and
shoulder length (there is nothing new in long hair for men!), he

wore a black frock coat, wing collar and black tie. By that time in his life he was becoming nearsighted, and he preached peering at his notes through his thick spectacles. But the whole congregation was held spellbound, not only at the tremendous message he was delivering but in waiting for the moments, every few minutes, when he would look up and smile at them all and his face literally shone with the glory of God. There was I sitting in the back row of the balcony, squeezed in among the great crowd, and in my backslidden state I would cry out to the Lord, "O God, that man has got what I want!"

Yes, there is a holy fear that falls upon the unbeliever and the backslider in the presence of a man of God. The sooner this is restored to our churches the better it will be for preacher and hearer alike, as the glory of God is revealed through the Word preached and the man who preaches, to create a hunger and thirst after righteousness on the part of all who listen: "And day by day continuing with one mind in the temple, and breaking bread from house to house, they were taking their meals together with gladness and sincerity of heart, praising God, and having favor with all the people" (Acts 2:46, 47).

Not only was there fear among the people, but the disciples also found favor with them. What a strange combination—fear and favor—but how wonderful! Persecution of the Church never came from the people but from the religious leaders, and that is always true. Counterfeit religion is always the greatest enemy of reality and truth.

A church full of Holy Spirit love flowing through to the world always has favor with the people. It does not have to seek their patronage! But once a church or a Christian loses the love of God flowing through, then that church or Christian has lost the people, because they have lost the magnetism of Calvary. It is when a church is in that situation that it will descend to any level in a frantic attempt to find an answer; but there is no substitute for Calvary love expressed through pastor and people.

Ah, but when love shines through, then the weary are strengthened; the lonely find fellowship; the defeated find hope; and the lost find Jesus! *That* is the influential church, and that is my burden for the worldwide Church today. For that is what will happen when revival comes: a Church from which suspicion, mistrust, coldness of heart, lack of confidence, and lovelessness have gone, departed for ever, to be replaced by love which brings fear and favor to all around, believer and unbeliever alike.

This is what happens on earth, and then there is something which happens in heaven:

> And the Lord added to their number day by day those who were being saved.
>
> Acts 2:47

> So then, those who had received his word were baptized; and there were added that day about three thousand souls.
>
> Acts 2:41

> And all the more believers in the Lord, multitudes of men and women, were constantly added to their number . . . .
>
> Acts 5:14

All these people were added to the Church, but primarily to the Lord Himself: *He* did it. It was not the eloquence or efficiency of the disciples, but He did it and added day by day to His own Body. And He will do it again today, wherever He can find a love-filled fellowship. The attitude of people is what it is today for lack of this. We have lost favor with them because we have lost the quality of love, and we have lost that because we have forgotten the meaning of true fellowship.

All this can be restored *now*—yes, today—not by some comment upon what has been said in this book, but by taking positive action to restore fellowship when it has been broken, to keep in rank with others, to sink personal preferences. Begin to use your home to meet your neighbors, chat to them about the Lord over a cup of tea or coffee; seek out ways to share His love and spread the news of salvation in His name. All this is possible only as, alone with God, you ask Him to shed abroad His love by the Holy Spirit in your heart.

Will you take action now, and so let the law of love in the power of the Holy Spirit be the fulfillment in and through your life of every demand that God can make upon you? If that happens, you will be one of those whom He can use to answer your own prayer for Holy Spirit revival.